Isaiah of Jerusalem

An Introduction

by

William J. Doorly

PAULIST PRESS
New York, N.Y./Mahwah, N.J.

*also from William J. Doorly
published by Paulist Press*

Prophet of Justice
Prophet of Love

Cover mosaic, *The Prophet Isaiah*, courtesy of Scala/Art Resource, NY.

The excerpt from *The New Jerome Biblical Commentary* edited by Raymond E. Brown, S.S., Joseph A. Fitzmyer, S.J. and Roland E. Murphy, O. Carm. is reprinted with the permission of the publisher, Prentice Hall, Inc. The excerpt from *Isaiah, The Eighth Century Prophet* by John Hayes and Stuart Irvine is reprinted with the permission of the publisher, Abingdon Press. The excerpt reprinted from *Reading Isaiah* by Edgar W. Conrad, copyright © 1991 Augsburg Fortress is used by permission. The excerpt from *Old Testament Parallels* by Victor H. Matthews and Don C. Benjamin is reprinted with the permission of the publisher, Paulist Press. Unless otherwise noted, the scripture quotations contained herein are from the New Revised Standard Version of the Bible, copyrighted 1989 by the Division of Christian Education of the National Council of the Churches of Christ in the United States of America, and are used by permission. All rights reserved.

Library of Congress Cataloging-in-Publication Data

Doorly, William J., 1931–
    Isaiah of Jerusalem: an introduction/by William J. Doorly.
      p. cm.
    Includes bibliographical references and index.
    ISBN 0-8091-3337-7
    1. Bible. O.T. Isaiah I-XXXIX—Study and teaching. I. Title.
  BS1515.5.D66 1992
  224'.106—dc20
                                       92-11648
                                         CIP

Published by Paulist Press
997 Macarthur Boulevard
Mahwah, New Jersey 07430

Printed and bound in the
United States of America

CONTENTS

Guide to Charts and Maps   v

Introduction   ix

Chapter 1   **The Role of the City of Jerusalem in the Emergence and Growth of First Isaiah**   1

Chapter 2   **The Prologue to the Book of Isaiah**   8

Chapter 3   **The Domination of the Near East by Assyria**   21

Chapter 4   **Early Oracles**   30

Chapter 5   **The Memoirs of Isaiah**   40

Chapter 6   **The Memoirs of Isaiah (Continued)**   50

Chapter 7   **The End of Isaiah's Early Prophetic Activity**   60

Chapter 8   **The Enthronement of a Prince of Peace**   69

Chapter 9   **A Shoot from the Stump of Jesse**   80

Chapter 10   **Oracles Concerning the Nations**   87

Chapter 11   **The Apocalypse of Isaiah**   97

CONTENTS

Chapter 12   **A Collection of Oracles**   108

Chapter 13   **Judgment and Salvation**   119

Chapter 14   **Historical Narratives of Isaiah and Hezekiah**   124

Chapter 15   **The Majestic Poet of the Exile (Second Isaiah)**   133

Chapter 16   **Third Isaiah: A Post-Exilic Collection**   143

Chapter 17   **The Unity of the Book of Isaiah**   150

                For Further Reading   158

                Index   160

GUIDE TO CHARTS AND MAPS

Divisions of the Book of Isaiah   xii

Chronology of Judah in the Days of Isaiah   xxiv

Parallels between the Book of Amos and Isaiah 1–5   16

The Assyrian Empire in the 8th and 7th Centuries B.C.   22

Kings of Assyria during Ministry of Isaiah   25

Major Events of Assyrian Interaction with Israel/Judah   28

The Seven Woe Statements   36

Ancient Palestine (Canaan)   41

Developments in the Syro-Ephraimitic Crisis   45

Last Six Kings of Israel, the Northern Kingdom   65

The Ancient Near East   98

Pattern of Alternating *Words of Judgment* and *Words of Hope* in Isaiah 28–33   109

An Example of Chiasm in Isaiah 28   110

Parallel Images from Second Isaiah Found in Chapter 35   121

Sennacherib's Attack on Jerusalem in 701   125

Prophetic Concepts and Poetic Images of First Isaiah   152

THIS BOOK IS DEDICATED TO THE MEMORY OF MY FATHER
WILLIAM HAMILTON DOORLY

INTRODUCTION

In this book we will be dealing primarily with the life, times, and oracles of Isaiah of Jerusalem who was the most influential of the four eighth century prophets, if not of all the Hebrew prophets. Isaiah's prophetic ministry is said to have lasted for approximately forty years from about 740 to 700 B.C.E. During this entire period, Assyria was the military power which ruthlessly dominated the entire area of Palestine and Syria. Her armies marched repeatedly from the east, from the area of Mesopotamia (modern day Iraq), destroying and laying waste with furious violence each of the small nations of the Near East, threatening the existence of Judah, Israel, and all of their neighbors, extracting precious resources from marginal nations which could hardly survive if left in peace.

The Divisions of the Book of Isaiah

We will briefly discuss the three sections of the canonical book of Isaiah as identified by scholars in modern times. The first section of Isaiah consists of chapters 1 to 39. All of the oracles of Isaiah of Jerusalem are found in this section,[1] which has as its background the Assyrian threat to Judah mentioned above, and the tremendous influence this threat had, on both the politics and economics of Judean leaders, and the theological pronouncements of Isaiah and the other eighth century prophets.

Section II of Isaiah begins in Chapter 40 and has as its background, *not* the constant threat of the Assyrian period (eighth century), but the events of the late Babylonian and early Persian period (late sixth century), along with the hope and faith which these changing events produced in the exilic, Judahite community of the Babylonian captivity.

As early as the fourteenth century C.E., a scholar by the name of Rabbi Abraham Ibn Ezra noted the difference in feeling and perspective which began with the opening of chapter 40:

> Comfort, O comfort my people,
>   says your God.
> Speak tenderly to Jerusalem and cry to her
>   that she has served her term,
>   that her penalty is paid,
> that she has received from the LORD's hand
>   double for all her sins (40:1).

For the student of Isaiah, beginning in chapter 40, Assyria abruptly disappears as the enemy of Judah. The destruction of Jerusalem is looked upon as an event of the past and a new day is dawning, a day filled with hope and faith for the people of Yahweh, renewal and restoration, peace and joy.

A return to Jerusalem for the captives is on the horizon. The previously defeated people of the Lord are about to receive new life:

> Those who wait for the LORD shall renew their strength,
>   they shall mount up with wings like eagles,
> they shall run and not be weary,
>   they shall walk and not faint (40:31).

We do not know the name of the author of chapters 40 through 55, this majestic poet of the late captivity, whose words introduce to us new and profound theological concepts which became the hearty blossoms of Hebrew theology, the seeds of which had been planted by the eighth century prophets, already a part of Israel's distant past.

A question which we must ask is this: Why were the oracles of the great unnamed prophet of the captivity (referred to by scholars as Second Isaiah or Deutero-Isaiah) included as an *extension* of the book which contained the oracles of Isaiah of Jerusalem?

It is an accepted fact that the oracles of all four of the eighth century prophets, Amos, Hosea, Micah, and Isaiah, were updated and enhanced by scribal redactors (who were prophets in their own right), both during the reign of King Josiah (640–609), and during the last decades of Judah's existence before the destruction of the temple and the city of Jerusalem. This important activity we refer to as the

Josianic redaction. A final period of editorial activity took place again during the latter days of the exile when it became obvious that the Persians were about to put an end to a century of Babylonian rule.

This late exilic redaction appears in all four eighth century prophetic books. In Hosea we read passages such as:

> The children of Israel shall return and seek the LORD their God, and David their king. . . . They shall return and dwell beneath my shadow, they shall flourish like a garden (Hos 3:5; 14:7).

All three divisions of the canonical book of Hosea end with a late-exilic redaction.[2]

At the conclusion of the book of Amos we have an exilic addition:

> I will restore the fortunes of my people Israel
>   and they shall rebuild the ruined cities and inhabit them;
> they shall plant vineyards and drink their wine.
>   and they shall make gardens and eat their fruit,
> I will plant them upon their land
>   and they shall never again be plucked up out of the land that I
>   have given them,
> says the LORD your God (Am 9:14–15).

If the oracles of Isaiah had received the same degree of redaction as Hosea, Amos, and Micah, Isaiah would still have been a much longer book. And indeed, there are similar exilic passages in the first 39 chapters of Isaiah.

However, the extension of the book of Isaiah beginning in chapter 40 is something much more than common redaction. The scroll of Isaiah obviously had a special place in the hearts of the exilic Judean community. Beginning with this generation, Isaiah's oracles received special treatment and attention. Their influence far exceeded that of the oracles of the other three eighth century prophets. This uniqueness of Isaiah's place in the collection of Hebrew scriptures continued in the Jewish community far beyond the exile. This was obviously true in the first century of the common era in the Essene community, and even more so among the followers of Jesus in the formation of the Christian scriptures. Scholars have identified almost six hundred references to sixty-three chapters of Isaiah in the Christian scriptures. There is no other book in the Hebrew Bible which comes close to this record.[3]

There are significant reasons for reading the oracles of Deutero-Isaiah as a continuation of the oracles of Isaiah of Jerusalem, and we will discuss these reasons in chapter 15 of our book, entitled "The Majestic Poet of the Exile."

The first extension of the scroll of Isaiah added fifteen chapters, but the scroll was still not complete. The oracles of Deutero-Isaiah concluded in chapter 55 with these words:

> For you shall go out in joy,
>   and be led back in peace;
> the mountains and the hills before you
>   shall burst into song,
> and all the trees of the field
>   shall clap their hands.
> Instead of the thorn shall come up the cypress;
>   instead of the brier shall come up the myrtle;
> and it shall be to the LORD for a memorial,
>   for an everlasting sign that shall not be cut off (55:12–13).

In the late nineteenth century a German scholar by the name of Bernhard Duhm was studying the canonical book of Isaiah when it became obvious to him that a third author (or group of authors) began

DIVISIONS OF THE BOOK OF ISAIAH

CHAPTERS	HISTORICAL PERIOD	AUTHOR(S)	LOCATION
1 to 39	Assyrian period with seventh century and sixth century redaction.	Isaiah of Jerusalem plus a Josianic and exilic redactor.	JERUSALEM AND BABYLON
40 to 55	Late Babylonian and early Persian period.	An unknown Judaic poet/ prophet of the exile.	BABYLON
56 to 66	Persian period (post-exilic).	The work of one or more post-exilic authors.	JERUSALEM

their contribution to the book of Isaiah in chapter 56. In a now famous book about Isaiah,[4] Duhm pointed out to scholars that a third distinct section of the book of Isaiah began with chapter 56. The mood and perspective of the book obviously changes for a third time, beginning with these words:

> Thus says the LORD:
> Maintain justice, and do what is right,
>   for soon my salvation will come,
>   and my deliverance be revealed.
> Happy is the mortal who does this,
>   the one who holds it fast,
> who keeps the sabbath, not profaning it,
>   and refrains from doing any evil (56:1-2).

Beginning in chapter 56 a new environment is obvious. We are back again in Jerusalem, a post-exilic Jerusalem which faced a variety of practical problems, in addition to the major problem of rebuilding the city and the temple of the Lord.

Although, in this volume, we will be dealing primarily only with the first division of the book of Isaiah, chapters 1 to 39, we will have occasion to refer to the remainder of the book. There is an obvious unity in the canonical version of Isaiah (all sixty-six chapters) which scholars have frequently discussed and illustrated. It is our belief that knowledge concerning the distinctiveness of the three divisions in no way diminishes our appreciation of the unity of the whole book. A good understanding of the birth and growth of the book can only increase our appreciation of the indigenous value of each section, and increase our understanding of the interrelationship of its parts, and how they contribute to a complex, but harmonious whole.

Coming to Terms with Multiple Authors

To expect that the Hebrew scroll named for the eighth century prophet Isaiah would have been the product of one author is to project into ancient Israel conditions and practices which did not exist. Individuals were not expected to produce books (scrolls) and be possessive about their content. Pride of authorship was not a factor. Those who came to be recognized as prophets spoke about situations which greatly concerned them because they had to. But individualism, such as that with which we are familiar in today's world, did not exist in ancient Israel. A person's identity was dependent on his or her membership in a group or community. Scrolls were the product of an ongoing community effort, and the period of development lasted for several centuries before the age of canonicity when the scrolls were declared to have reached their final form.

The Role of Liturgy

As social and political situations changed drastically in ancient Judah (the southern kingdom), scribes and priests would take the oracles of an established prophet, such as Amos or Isaiah, and produce an updated scroll to address religious and social problems of a new age. The oracles of the original prophet would be embellished and reinterpreted and, finally, lovingly placed in a new structure. Very often the purpose of the new structure was liturgical. These scrolls were not updated to be put on a shelf for scholars. The new scroll was produced to be read and presented to public gatherings of Judahites, to glorify Yahweh and to educate his people.

The Changing Audience

One of the problems produced by this process of growth has to do with the changing addressees. The eighth century oracles were pretty much addressed to the powerful elite of Samaria and Jerusalem. The expanded scrolls of the Josianic period were addressed to a larger, more general audience, including the masses of Judah. This was part of the effort to centralize and standardize the religion of Yahweh in Judah, controlled by Jerusalem. In summary, this is what happened. The original oracles of the eighth century addressed specific groups within society, namely the powerful decision makers of the two capital cities. The first major expansions of the original oracles addressed a different religious and social situation in Judah and were produced to include a wider audience including the people at large. When the people went into captivity, the scrolls went with them and the process continued.

The book of Isaiah in the Hebrew Bible, with its variety of majestic and powerful passages, is based on the oracles of the eminent eighth century prophet Isaiah of Jerusalem. Isaiah had many things in common with the other three eighth century prophets whose oracles form the basis for books of prophecy which carry their names. They were:

Amos of Tekoa,
Hosea ben Beeri,
Micah of Moresheth.

Like those prophets, Isaiah was zealous for Yahweh, the champion God of ancient Israel. Like Amos and Micah, Isaiah was disturbed by the exploitation of the masses of Yahweh's people by the powerful elite of the capital cities, Samaria and Jerusalem. Like Hosea, Isaiah looked on political alliances with Assyria and Egypt as a betrayal and denial of an ancient relationship between Israel and Yahweh.

But Isaiah of Jerusalem was unique among the eighth century prophets. We can cite some of these obvious differences even before we begin a study of his oracles.

(1) Isaiah is the only eighth century prophet appearing in the Bible History (Deuteronomistic History, and the Chronicles history).[5] Interactions between King Hezekiah and Isaiah are reported in 2 Kings 19–20. In the Bible history there are a number of conversations recorded between *non-literary* prophets (prophets who did not write books and who do not have books of prophecy based on their oracles in the canonical version of the Hebrew Bible), and kings, or persons who later became kings. These recorded conversations are characteristic of the Deuteronomistic History (DH). Some examples are:

a. Samuel speaks with King Saul. (1 Sam 15:12–31)
b. Samuel anoints David. (1 Sam 16:11–13)
c. Nathan speaks with King David. (2 Sam 7:1–17)
d. Ahijah speaks with Jeroboam. (1 Kgs 11:29–35)
e. Shemaiah speaks with Rehoboam. (1 Kgs 12:21–24)
f. Elijah speaks with King Ahab. (1 Kgs 18:14–19)

None of the above five prophets were literary prophets however. Their oracles do not form the basis for a Hebrew[6] book of prophecy. Other than Isaiah, the other three eighth century literary prophets, Amos, Hosea, and Micah, are not mentioned in DH, or the much later Chronicler's history.[7]

(2) Whereas the oracles of Amos, Hosea, and Micah in their final form were short enough to share a scroll with nine other prophetic books, the canonical book bearing Isaiah's name needed a large scroll just for itself. In English translation the final book of Isaiah is sixty-six

chapters, making it the longest book in the Hebrew Bible except for the book of Psalms.[8]

(3) Isaiah is the only eighth century prophet who lived in Jerusalem. This is important because it was in Jerusalem during the reign of Josiah, a century after the activity of the eighth century prophets, that the oracles of the four (Amos, Hosea, Micah, and Isaiah) were selected for scribal activity, producing the important seventh century scrolls containing editorial expansions and enhancements of the earlier copies of their oracles. This process of editorial activity is called redaction, a term which we will be using repeatedly in this study and which we will discuss below. This updating was for the purpose of interpreting the original oracles for application to a completely new situation facing Judah during the reign of Josiah.[9] The seventh century redactional process was carried out by a group of scribes and priests who were zealous for Yahweh, and who had as a goal the standardization and centralization of Yahwism in Jerusalem, ". . . the place which Yahweh chose, to make his name dwell" (Deut 12:11). In chapter 1 we will discuss in greater detail how the fact that Isaiah lived in Jerusalem may have influenced the unique growth of his oracles.

The Several Authors of Isaiah

Modern scholarship has determined another unique difference between Isaiah and the other three eighth century prophets. If the book of Isaiah had reached its completed form as a result of the same type of redaction and expansion which the books of Amos, Hosea, and Micah received, the book of Isaiah would have ended with chapter 33. All of the oracles of Isaiah of Jerusalem are found in the first thirty-three chapters.[10]

This means that we have to account for six chapters (34 through 39) which appear before the start of the second division of the canonical book (chapters 40 through 55), the late exilic oracles of Deutero-Isaiah.

Here we meet our first complication in studying and understanding the first part of the book of Isaiah. It would be easier for us if we were able to assume that the first thirty-nine chapters came chronologically first, then the second section (40–55), the oracles of Deutero-Isaiah, then the third section (chapters 56–66), the oracles of Trito-Isaiah. Unfortunately this is an assumption which we cannot make. Most scholars have found parts of the first thirty-nine chapters which have been influenced by Deutero-Isaiah, or at least to be exilic in origin. What this means is that the first thirty-nine chapters did not exist as a complete scroll in its present form before chapters 40 through 55 were appended to it. The growth of the first part of the book is a complicated story. To understand this story we must review some facts about the manner in which the first prophetic books of the Hebrew Bible grew and developed.

The eighth century prophetic books can be described as collections of divine poetry from different stages in the lives of the prophets and from different stages in the life of Israel and Judah. Each of the books which carry the name of an eighth century prophet reached its final form after going through a long period of development. Simply stated the stages were these:

A. The original oracles of Isaiah (and Amos, Hosea, and Micah) were updated and enlarged during the reign of Josiah (640–609), and this activity is referred to as the Josianic redaction.

B. Almost a century later, late in the captivity, the Josianic scrolls were subject to a final redaction (editorial updating) which reflected a newly restored faith and hope of the Judaic community in captivity.

Stages and Characteristics of the Josianic Redaction

1. Four eighth century prophets spoke for Yahweh, the ancient God of Israel, critical of decisions made by the leaders of Israel and Judah in the capital cities of Samaria and Jerusalem. This took place from 750 to 700 B.C.E.

2. One hundred years later, during the reign of King Josiah (640–609), the four scrolls containing the oracles of these prophets, Amos, Hosea, Isaiah, and Micah, were updated and enlarged.

3. The truth carried by the written words of the eighth century prophets was appropriated by a group of zealous champions of Yahweh who considered themselves to be descendants of an ancient order of priests known as Levites.[11]

4. The eighth century oracles of each prophet appeared in a new, more complicated theological structure which addressed the theological concerns of these priests and reflected their goal of the standardization and centralization of the religion of Yahweh in Jerusalem.

5. The enhancement and enlargement of a scroll containing oracles from an earlier time is referred to as redaction.

6. Redaction was not carried on in a light-handed way. It was a process which required great skill and seriousness, and its procedures have been critically analyzed and explained by scholars in a variety of studies available to us in Bible commentaries and special studies.[12]

7. Although we sometimes refer to the Josianic redactor as a person it is more likely that the work was accomplished by a circle of scribes and priests who were obedient servants of Yahweh.

8. This circle of scribes and priests had the greatest respect for the oracles of the eighth century prophets. It is possible that apart from their seventh century redactional activity we may not have had the eighth century oracles preserved for us.

9. These enlarged editions of the seventh century oracles became part of a public liturgy. The purpose of the liturgy was for the practical purpose of teaching and indoctrinating the people. The liturgies consisted of readings by the scribes and priests at public gatherings. These liturgies may have included songs and chants which are now part of the prophetic books.

So, the original oracles had introductions and conclusions added to them, hymnic material interspersed throughout, and "congregational responses" strategically placed. We can now recognize that these Josianic redactors were the first liturgists of our Judaic-Christian tradition.

10. Because the oracles of the earlier prophets were collections, they were not always placed in chronological order. To the modern reader this presents a difficulty. We like to have things in logical order, with first things first. You do not find this in the so-called eighth century prophetic books. These collections are more akin to works of great art, or orchestral music, where themes are introduced, sometimes to be dropped suddenly, and later reintroduced and developed.

Exilic Redaction

With the final destruction of the city of Jerusalem and the temple by the Babylonians in 586 the only treasures which the Judahites had left were the writings of the Josianic age and the last decades of Judah. These they were able to carry into captivity. During exile the Judahites became "people of the book." By small groups these scrolls were read, studied, memorized and adored. One of the scrolls contained the Josianic edition of the oracles of Isaiah.

The second half of the sixth century, following forty years of exile for a sizable Judaic community, was a period of redaction for the Josianic scrolls. These included at least the following: the book of Deuteronomy, the Deuteronomistic History, and the four books of the eighth century prophets.

The Josianic scroll of Isaiah received the same kind of serious editorial updating and enhancement as the scrolls of Amos, Hosea, and Micah. There was a difference for Isaiah, however. First, the oracles of Isaiah had grown to a length which exceeded the length of Amos, Hosea, and Micah put together. Second, the other three eighth century prophets reached their final form during the exile, whereas Isaiah was still to grow.

It is possible that the prophet known as Deutero-Isaiah completed his composition (chapters 40 to 55 of Isaiah) before the final redaction of the first thirty-nine chapters took place. It is also possible that Deutero-Isaiah may have taken part in the exilic redaction of the first thirty-nine chapters of Isaiah. We do not know for sure. We have no information concerning this period. We can only speculate.

There are passages in the first section of Isaiah, particularly chapter 35, which sound very much like Deutero-Isaiah.

Strengthen the weak hands,
   and make firm the feeble knees.
Say to those who are of a fearful heart,
   "Be strong, do not fear!
Here is your God. He will come with vengeance,
   with terrible recompense.
He will come and save you.

Then the eyes of the blind will be opened,
   and the ears of the deaf unstopped;
then the lame shall leap like a deer,
   and the tongue of the speechless sing for joy.
For waters shall break forth in the wilderness,
   and streams in the desert;
the burning sand shall become a pool,
   and the thirsty ground springs of water (35:5–7).

So the scroll of Isaiah was considered special by the scribes of the exilic community and grew to a length much longer than the other three prophets of the eighth century. When Amos, Hosea, and Micah

reached their final, canonical form, the canon of Isaiah was still open
for growth. As we have explained, Isaiah did not reach its final form
until the period of rebuilding and restoration which followed the
return of Yahweh's chastened people to a Jerusalem in ruins:

> So I came to Jerusalem and was there for three days. . . . I
> went out by night by the Valley Gate past the Dragon's
> Spring and to the Dung Gate, and I inspected the walls of
> Jerusalem that had been broken down and its gates which
> had been destroyed by fire. Then I went on to the Fountain
> Gate and to the King's Pool: but there was no place for the
> animal I was riding to continue. . . . Then I said to them,
> "You see the trouble we are in, how Jerusalem lies in ruins
> with its gates burned. Come let us rebuild the wall of Jerusa-
> lem, so that we may no longer suffer disgrace" (Neh 2:
> 11–14, 17).

During this period of rebuilding, the scroll of Isaiah was read and
studied by a group of priests and scribes, and the last division was
added to the scroll, chapters 56 through 66, containing the oracles of
a prophet whom scholars have called Trito-Isaiah or Third Isaiah.

What was unique about the oracles of Isaiah of Jerusalem which
caused them to be treated differently than the oracles of the other
three eighth century prophets, causing them to provide the basis for
the longest and most influential book of Hebrew prophecy? We will
turn to this question in Chapter 1.

How To Use This Book as a Study Guide

(a) At the beginning of each chapter, recommended scriptural
readings are identified. It is important to read these recommended
chapters.

(b) At the end of each chapter there are Study Questions. In
most cases, but not every case, the answer to the question will be
found in the text of the chapter. Occasionally the answer will be
found in the notes.

(c) Notes for each chapter have been supplied. They have been
planned to provide additional information and concepts which will be
of assistance to the serious student.

STUDY QUESTIONS

1. Describe the three sections of the book of Isaiah identified by biblical scholars.

2. What were the three national military powers which dominated the area of the fertile crescent during the development of the book of Isaiah? What was the relationship of Judah to these three powers?

3. Why did priests and scribes of a later age put the oracles of Isaiah into a liturgical framework?

4. Discuss the difference between the audience of the eighth century prophetic oracles and the audience of the seventh century updated oracles.

5. What are the names of the four eighth century prophets?

6. How is Isaiah similar to the other three eighth century prophets?

7. Even before identifying and studying the oracles of Isaiah, what are three unique things we can say about him?

8. What does the term "redaction" mean? What does the term redactor mean?

9. What are two most likely periods of redaction for the eighth century prophets?

10. Who were the redactors of the Josianic edition of the eighth century prophets?

NOTES

1. The oracles of Isaiah of Jerusalem are actually found in the first thirty-three chapters of Isaiah. We will discuss chapters 34 and 35 in our chapter 13, entitled "Judgment and Salvation." The four narrative chapters dealing with Isaiah and Hezekiah, chapters 36 to 39, were added to the book a century or more after the events to which they refer. Please see our chapter 14, "Historical Narratives of Isaiah and Hezekiah."

2. See the dissertation by Gale A. Yee entitled *Composition and Tradition in the Book of Hosea: A Redactional Critical Investigation* (New York: Scholars Press, 1987).

3. See the article "Isaiah in Luke" by James A. Sanders in *Interpretation*, April 1982, Volume XXXVI, number 2.

4. Bernhard Duhm, *Das Buch Jesaja* (Göttingen: Vanderhoecj and Ruprecht, 1892, 1902).

5. There are two histories of Israel in the Hebrew Bible. The earliest is called by scholars the Deuteronomic or Deuteronomistic History. It is frequently referred to in scholarly works as DH. First identified in modern times by Martin Noth, it consists of the books of Joshua, Judges, Samuel, and Kings. The first edition of the Deuteronomistic History appeared in the days of Josiah and ended with Josiah as the perfect servant of Yahweh. The final (canonical) edition of DH was much longer. It added information about the kings following Josiah, and added several theological explanations for the reasons why Yahweh permitted the destruction of Jerusalem in 597 (and completely in 586) by the Babylonians, and the theological purpose of the captivity.

Isaiah is also mentioned in the Chronicles history (2 Chr 32) which is a much later history based partly on the earlier DH.

6. We use the word Hebrew to refer to the language of ancient Israel and Judah. It is not correct to refer to the citizens of ancient Israel or Judah as "Hebrews" as has often been done in books about the Hebrew Bible.

7. The second history in the Hebrew Bible is found in 1 and 2 Chronicles. It was compiled centuries later than the Deuteronomistic History (Joshua, Judges, Samuel, Kings), and is dependent upon the earlier history to some degree. The relationship of the two histories is a complex area of study in itself.

8. In an English translation Hosea consists of nine pages, Amos, seven pages, and Micah, six pages. Because of their short length they are called minor prophets. Isaiah in its canonical (final) form consists of fifty-four pages and in ancient times needed a complete scroll for itself. Because of its length Isaiah is called a major prophet.

9. Before the days of Josiah there was no widespread understanding that Yahweh would communicate with his people through written scrolls. The discovery of the book of the law in the temple in 621 B.C.E. is the first mention of the recognition of a written scroll as the word of Yahweh. The scribes and priests who produced DH were pioneers in using the written word as a revelation from God in Israel. When the first version of DH was complete, ending with Josiah as the

ideal servant of Yahweh and leader of his people, the same circle redacted (edited, updated, and enhanced) the oracles of four eighth century prophets. This may mean that the Hebrew Bible in its earliest form consisted of the first edition of DH, plus the four seventh century editions of the four prophets, with an early version of Deuteronomy serving as a preface.

10. Many scholars believe that chapters 34 and 35 of Isaiah, sometimes referred to as "the little apocalypse," are not the work of Isaiah and were added much later. The historical narrative of Isaiah and King Hezekiah, chapters 36–39, was not written by Isaiah and was added to the collection of Isaiah's oracles sometime during the captivity. See for example pages 372–376 in the book by John Hayes and Stuart Irvine, *Isaiah, the Eighth Century Prophet* (Nashville: Abingdon, 1987).

11. The zealous levitical priests and scribes which I refer to here are commonly referred to by scholars as the Deuteronomists. In the book of Deuteronomy the only priests mentioned are assumed to be Levites.

12. For a complete study of the detailed redaction of a book of eighth century prophecy see Gale Yee's book based on her dissertation entitled *Composition and Tradition in the Book of Hosea: A Redaction Critical Investigation* (New York: Scholars Press, 1987). For a simpler study see my book on Amos, *Prophet of Justice*, or my book on Hosea, *Prophet of Love*, both published by Paulist Press.

CHRONOLOGY OF JUDAH IN THE DAYS OF ISAIAH

791[1]   Uzziah becomes king of Judah.

750   Uzziah is stricken with leprosy. Jotham, his son, becomes co-regent.

745   Assyria begins to reorganize in the east with eyes on conquest of the Mediterranean area.

739   Uzziah dies. Jotham becomes sole king. Isaiah has his vision of Yahweh in the temple.

736   King Jotham dies. Ahaz becomes king of Judah.

735   Israel and Syria begin to pressure Ahaz to join the anti-Assyrian coalition.

734   The port of Elath is taken from Judah by Edom.

734–33   Tiglath-pileser captures Damascus and subdues Israel.

722   Assyria destroys Samaria, putting an end to Israel, the northern kingdom. Sargon completes the capture of Samaria started by Shalmanesser.

715   Hezekiah becomes sole king of Judah. He may have been co-regent before this date.

705   Sargon II dies leading troops against Anatolia. The nations of Syria/Palestine rejoice. Hezekiah is a leader of rebellion against Assyria.

701   Sennacherib attacks Judah, destroying forty-six cities. Hezekiah pays heavy tribute to Sennacherib. Jerusalem is threatened by Sennacherib but is not captured. After returning home Sennacherib is murdered and Esarhaddon becomes king of Assyria.

---

1. There is no universal agreement for many of these dates. For example, the *New Jerome Biblical Commentary* gives 783 as the date for the beginning of Uzziah's reign. Hayes and Hooker in their *New Chronology* give 785. The *Interpreter's One Volume Bible Commentary* gives 791.

Chapter 1

THE ROLE OF THE CITY OF JERUSALEM IN THE EMERGENCE AND GROWTH OF FIRST ISAIAH

Suggested Scripture Readings:

Isaiah 7:1–9
Isaiah 37:1–7
Isaiah 38:1–8

Isaiah was the only eighth century literary prophet to live in Jerusalem. In exploring the reasons for the growth of Isaiah's oracles we cannot ignore the role which Jerusalem played in the special treatment which his oracles received, both in Josianic times, and later, during the exile and following the exile.

Historical and Theological Developments in Jerusalem

(1) Jerusalem was the capital city which survived for more than a hundred years after the destruction of the northern kingdom, Israel, and the destruction of Samaria, its capital city.

(2) Jerusalem was the place where priests and scribes of the north fled, especially from the Shechem/Shiloh area, following the invasion of Israel by the Assyrians in the latter part of the eighth century.

(3) Jerusalem was the place where theological questions (and

1

answers) raised by the destruction of the northern kingdom were generated.

(4) Jerusalem was the place where written scrolls were first recognized as containing the words of Yahweh (2 Kgs 22:11–16).

(5) Jerusalem was the home of the *Deuteronomists* where the scrolls of the eighth century prophets were edited and updated to become the first prophetic books of the Hebrew Bible.

(6) Jerusalem was the place where the great pre-exilic and post-exilic prophets lived.

(7) Jerusalem was the home of the exilic Judahite community, and the city to which they returned to rebuild.

(8) Jerusalem was the location of the temple. It was the place which Yahweh had chosen ". . . for his name to dwell."

(9) Jerusalem was the place envisioned by the exilic and post-exilic prophets as being the center of Yahweh's plan for the future of mankind.

If we ask the question, "Was there something unique about the oracles of Isaiah which caused them to grow into the longest book of the Hebrew Bible?" we have to be honest in our answer. All four of the eighth century prophets were unique. The oracles of each one have their own characteristics and values. As stated above, the central importance of Jerusalem in the formation of the scriptures must be kept in mind, particularly in analyzing the subsequent growth of the book of Isaiah; having Jerusalem as his home base was a factor.

As we proceed with our study of Isaiah it will be helpful for us to keep these two things in mind:

1. In the days of Isaiah, there was no single authorized theological viewpoint throughout Israel and Judah. There were diverse *theologies*.

2. The eighth century prophets were political conservatives who promoted values of Israel's ancient past and who championed dependence on Yahweh, the ancient warrior God of Israel.

Theological Diversity in Eighth Century Israel and Judah

A century after Isaiah there was a movement to standardize and centralize the religion of Yahweh in Jerusalem. At that time the territory of Yahweh's people had been greatly reduced. In the century past Judahites had witnessed the reduction and the final destruction of their sister nation to the north, Israel, by several great Assyrian kings, culminating in the tragic events of 722.

In 701, Judah itself had been ravished by the forces of Sennacherib. In his annals he claims to have destroyed forty-six towns and fortresses of Judah. His records of the destruction of Lachish, the second largest city of Judah, are vividly recorded on an outstanding series of reliefs from Nineveh, now on display at the British Museum.

The effort of centralization and unification attempted in the reign of Josiah could not have existed in the days of Isaiah, however. In the eighth century, when the territory of Israel/Judah was much larger and more diverse, there was no central, *authorized* form of Yahwism. There were territorial differences which scholars refer to under the heading of "local traditions." These locations included, but were certainly not limited to, Shechem, Shiloh, Bethel, Hebron and Beersheba.[1] With Israel divided into two distinct political entities, Israel in the north, and Judah in the south, there had to have been at least two forms of Yahwism. But there was another division among the people of ancient Israel which we must not forget. There was a great gap between the urban and rural populations also. And this brings us into the field of sociology.[2]

The Feeling of Marginality in Pre-Monarchical Israel

We have stated that the eighth century prophets were political conservatives who found their values in Israel's past and championed dependence on Yahweh, the ancient warrior God of Israel.

We must never forget that the religion of early Israel had deep roots in its feelings of marginality. Citizens of pre-monarchical Israel knew that they were not the influential, the rich or the powerful. This is preserved for us in several scriptural traditions. Israel is not included in the Table of the Nations in Genesis 10 (an ancient table used by the priestly editor/author in his compilation of Genesis), and in Deuteronomy 7:7 Israel is reminded:

> It was not because you were more in number than any other people that the LORD set his love upon you and chose you, for you were the fewest of all people.

In Numbers we have this interesting description:

> . . . a people dwelling alone, and not reckoning itself among the nations (23:8–9).

And we must not forget the plea in the book of Amos:

How can Jacob stand? He is so small (7:2,5).

Pre-monarchical Israel was a poor, second class nation, if it could be called a nation at all. This Israel needed a strong, protective God, and it found that God in Yahweh, a champion of marginal people. This was the Yahweh who led the Hebrews out of Egypt, and the Hebrews were people who gave meaning to the term marginality. With the capture of the city of Jerusalem by the army of David, however, a new form of Yahwism was about to emerge. Religious values associated with marginality would continue to survive in rural areas such as Shechem and Shiloh, but in Jerusalem a new pride and feeling of superiority would arise which would affect ancient perceptions of Yahweh as a God of the under-classes.

The Royal Theology

With the coming of the monarchy, especially during the reign of Solomon, a new class of Israelite came into existence, a rich, elite, urban class. Unfortunately this new urban class prospered at the expense of rural peasants and farmers of Israel. Decisions made by the powerful of Jerusalem and Samaria were frequently not in the best interests of the rural poor. The masses were exploited by the urban elite for the purpose of strengthening the monarchy. Values of a former time were discarded, along with the dependent, trustful relationship with Yahweh, as the sole protector of Israel.

In Jerusalem, a new perception of Yahweh emerged as a God who chose to dwell in the holy of holies, as a resident of the royal sanctuary. This Yahweh had an agreement with the house of David to protect it and cause it to flourish in perpetuity.

You [the LORD] said,
"I have made a covenant with my chosen one.
    I have sworn to my servant David:
'I will establish your descendants forever,
    and build your throne for all generations.' . . .
I will not lie to David.
His line shall continue forever
    and his throne endure before me like the sun" (Ps 89:3–4,
    36–37).

The theological elements of the cult of Yahweh in Jerusalem which deal with the special blessings of Yahweh for the house of David are referred to by scholars as the *royal* theology, and sometimes as the *Davidic* theology. It cannot be underestimated as a contributing factor to the religion of ancient Judah and the emergence of the Hebrew scriptures.

The Zion Tradition

As powerful as the *royal* theology was in distinguishing a Jerusalemite form of Yahwism from rural forms of Israelite religion, it was not the only factor that we have to keep in mind in understanding the oracles of Isaiah of Jerusalem. Pre-dating the royal theology of the house of David was a Jerusalem tradition with strong mythological roots which *pre-dated* the capture of Jerusalem by David. Notice in the following excerpts from the Psalms that there is no specific mention of the House of David:

There is a river whose streams make glad the city of God,
    the holy habitation of the most High
God is in the midst of her,
    she shall not be moved (Ps 46:4–5).

Great is the LORD
    and greatly to be praised in the city of our God!
His holy mountain, beautiful in elevation,
    is the joy of the whole earth,
Mount Zion in the far north,
    the city of the great King.
Within her citadels God has shown himself a sure defense. . . .
As we have heard,
    so have we seen in the city of the LORD of hosts,
in the city of our God,
    which God establishes forever (Ps 48:1–3,8).

For the LORD has chosen Zion;
    he has desired it for his habitation:
"This is my resting place for ever;
    here I will dwell for I have desired it . . ." (Ps 132:13–14).

Combining the royal, Davidic theology and the ancient Jebusite

(Zion) traditions concerning special protection for the city of Salem, with the belief that Yahweh had chosen Jerusalem for his dwelling place, a new form of urban Yahwism appeared which distinguished itself from the various rural forms of the religion of Israel and Judah.

Summary

In comparing the environment of Isaiah with the other three eighth century prophets, it is reasonable to consider the special role which Jerusalem played, both in the eighth century, when the oracles were first conceived and delivered, and in the subsequent handling of these oracles by the scribes and priests who may have considered themselves disciples or followers of Isaiah in the days of King Josiah and during the final years of the Babylonian captivity.

STUDY QUESTIONS

1. What were some of the historical and theological developments which took place in Jerusalem following the destruction of the northern kingdom?

2. Was there an authorized form of Yahwism, accepted by all Israel in the days of Isaiah? Discuss.

3. What do we mean by *a feeling of marginality* in early Israel?

4. What is meant by the royal theology?

5. What is meant by the Zion tradition, and how does it differ from the royal theology?

6. Is it reasonable to suspect that the environment of Isaiah (Jerusalem) would cause him to have a different perspective than the other three eighth century prophets? Explain.

NOTES

1. For example some scholars have discovered patriarchal traditions in different locations. Hebron had traditions of Abraham, Bethel of Jacob, and Beersheba of Isaac.

2. In this volume we are not going to enter into a lengthy discussion of the sociology of the early prophetic period and how this approach assists us in understanding the eighth century prophets. See my Paulist Press book *Prophet of Justice* for a discussion of the importance of the sociological approach to a prophetic book.

Chapter 2

THE PROLOGUE TO
THE BOOK OF ISAIAH

Suggested Scripture Reading:

Isaiah 1

We call the first chapter of Isaiah the prologue for two reasons. It is a collection of oracles which serves as a preface for the book, and the collection is separated from the rest of the book by an earlier title in chapter 2:1:

> The word that Isaiah son of Amoz saw concerning Judah and Jerusalem (2:1).

A longer title for the book is found in the opening verse of chapter 1:

> The vision of Isaiah son of Amoz, which he saw concerning Judah and Jerusalem in the days of Uzziah, Jotham, Ahaz, and Hezekiah, kings of Judah (1:1).

The title found in chapter 2 is an earlier title for an earlier written version of the oracles of Isaiah of Jerusalem. We used the word *earlier* twice in the previous sentence to make a point. In reading a book of the Hebrew Bible, the first verse, or verses, encountered by the reader may be the last part of the book to be written. It was the practice of scribes and the circles of which they were an integral part to add introductions and opening material to an older written document. The scribes and priests who handled these scrolls took their work very seriously. The words of introductions were carefully chosen to assist the reader in understanding the book and often had profound theological implications.

So what the modern reader encounters first in reading a book of the Bible, sometimes a title verse, and sometimes an entire chapter or more, can often be dated later than the text which follows. For example, scholars agree that the first chapter of the book of Genesis is much later than the older opening which began in Genesis 2:4:

> In the day that the LORD God made the earth and the heavens . . . then the LORD God made man out of the dust of the earth (Gen 2:4,7).

Also, there are two introductions to the book of Deuteronomy. The introduction in Deuteronomy 4:44 is the first verse of an earlier edition than the canonical book of Deuteronomy:[1]

> This is the law that Moses set before the Israelites (Deut 4:44).

When we study the eighth century prophets we can assume that the title found in the opening verse was added much later than the delivery of the oracles and the first written record of the oracles.

The first word of the book of Isaiah is "vision." This may be significant. This word does not appear in the title verse for Amos, Hosea, or Micah.[2] Seeing, and the inability to see, is a theme which runs throughout the book of Isaiah. In the year that King Uzziah died (739 B.C.E.), Isaiah *saw* the Lord. He was in the temple, presumably with other people, but they saw nothing. Metaphors built on the senses of hearing and seeing run throughout the three sections of the book. Isaiah hears God speaking to him:

> Make the mind of this people dull,
>   and stop their ears,
>   and shut their eyes,
> so that they may not look with their eyes,
>   and listen with their ears . . . (6:10).

A later contributor to the book will predict the day when ". . . the eyes of the blind shall be opened" (35:5), and Deutero-Isaiah will write that the servant of the LORD will ". . . open the eyes that are blind" (42:7).

Yahweh's People Stand Accused

Like a lawyer or a person bringing suit in a court of law, the author brings charges against Judah calling on heaven and earth as witnesses:

> I reared children and brought them up,
>   but they have rebelled against me.
> The ox knows its owner,
>   and the donkey its master's crib;
> but Israel does not know,
>   my people do not understand (Is 1:2–3).

Accusations like this are common in the books of prophecy. Here are two examples from Amos and Hosea:

> They do not know how to do right, says the LORD,
> those who store up violence in their strongholds (Am 3:10).

> There is no faithfulness or loyalty,
>   and no knowledge of God in the land (Hos 4:1).

Would it have been better to start the book on a more positive note? Unfortunately that's not what the eighth century prophets are all about. If we had to describe the activity of the eighth century prophets in a few words, we could say that they were angry messengers who brought charges against the leaders of God's people. The angry oracles are directed against the leaders of the people, those who are in positions of power, those who make decisions in the capital cities, princes, priests, and judges. Hosea had said:

> Hear this, O priests!
>   Give heed, O house of Israel!
> Hearken, O house of the king!
>   For the judgment pertains to you (5:1–2).

In the prologue Isaiah will say:

Hear the word of the LORD, you rulers of Sodom (1:10).

And later:

Your princes are rebels and companions of thieves.
  Everyone loves a bribe and runs after gifts.
They do not defend the orphan,
  and the widow's cause does not come before them (1:23).

The Holy One of Israel

Starting in verse 4, the author comments on the Lord's accusation and adds his own words of accusation, charging the nation with despising ". . . the Holy One of Israel." This title for Judah's God is found frequently in the book of Isaiah, and has been called by some commentators Isaiah's favorite title for the God of Judah. Other scholars have stated that it is the center of Isaiah's theology.

The word "Israel" attests to the title's ancient origin. In Isaiah's time Israel was the name of the northern kingdom, but centuries earlier, in pre-monarchical Israel, and in the early days of the monarchy during the reigns of Saul, David, and Solomon, it was the name of all the people, including the state of Judah.

It certainly is a key phrase, contributing to the interrelationship of the three divisions of the book of Isaiah. In First Isaiah the title appears twelve times and in Second Isaiah it appears thirteen times.[3] The title does not appear in the original oracles of the other eighth century prophets. The reason for this may lie in the fact that this ancient title was used in the Jerusalem cult of Yahweh. We will discuss its significance when we reach Isaiah's vision of Yahweh in the temple (Isaiah 6).

Judgment Has Devastated the Country

God has punished the nation, but the leaders have not returned to Yahweh.[4]

Your country lies desolate,
  your cities are burned with fire;
in your very presence
  aliens devour your land;
  it is desolate, as overthrown by foreigners.

And daughter Zion is left like a booth in a vineyard,
　　like a shelter in a cucumber field,
　　like a besieged city.
If the LORD of hosts had not left us a few survivors
　　we would have been like Sodom,
　　and become like Gomorrah (Is 1:7–9).

And this brings us to our first problem. What catastrophe is referred to in the above words? There are three separate historical possibilities presented by noted scholars, and a short review of the three answers is in order.

(a) John Hayes and Stuart Irvine in a recent commentary on Isaiah[5] state that the catastrophe referred to in chapter 1 of Isaiah was the earthquake mentioned in Amos 1:1 (". . . two years before the earthquake"), and in Zechariah 14:5:

　　. . . and you shall flee as you fled from the earthquake in the
　　days of King Uzziah of Judah.

In the Hays-Irvine commentary the prophetic activity of Isaiah is said to have started around 745 B.C.E. The date for the earthquake is given as 748.[6]

The authors state that the description of the condition of the land beginning in verse 7, "Your country lies desolate, your cities are burned with fire," refers to the aftermath of the earthquake and does not refer to the results of an invasion of the land by a foreign military power. Verse 7 of the RSV which reads:

　　. . . in your very presence aliens devour your land;
　　it is desolate, as overthrown by foreigners (1:7),

is translated differently by the authors. The words *aliens* and *foreigners* are translated as *trespassers*, and in the commentary are referred to as *looters* and *outsiders*. The mention of Sodom and Gomorrah was appropriate because it spoke to what the readers considered the "most disastrous of calamities."[7]

(b) Roland E. Clements in his commentary on Isaiah 1–39[8] states that the situation described in Isaiah, chapter 1 is certainly the invasion of Judah by the Assyrian king Sennacherib. In 701 Sennacherib boasted of destroying forty-six villages and towns of Judah before threatening Jerusalem, holding Hezekiah as a prisoner in "his royal city."[9] This view, that the catastrophe referred to is the 701 invasion by Sennacherib, is also presented in *The New Jerome Biblical Commentary*.[10] Clements comments that the mention of "few survivors" in verse 9 was added much later to allow the passage to refer to the tragic events of the last Babylonian invasion of Jerusalem in 587.

(c) Otto Kaiser, in his commentary *Isaiah 1–12*,[11] states that the historical context is the great catastrophe of 587, the final destruction of Jerusalem by the Babylonians:

> . . . a servant of the king of Babylon . . . burned down the house of the LORD, the king's house, and all the houses of Jerusalem; every great house he burned down. All the army of the Chaldeans who were with the captain of the guard broke down the walls around Jerusalem (2 Kgs 25:9–10).

So here we have an example of three scholars who do not agree on an interpretation of a very concrete piece of scripture. Some questions may come to our mind. If the earthquake was so devastating, why is there no description of its aftermath or even a mention of it in the Bible histories? If the third answer is correct, that the devastation refers to the events of 587, why is there no language in the oracle speaking of the destruction of the house of Yahweh, certainly a very significant theological concern?

Ultimately, there may be no correct, accessible answer. Since we have identified chapter 1 as a prologue, it may have been shaped to deal with general theological themes for which greater detail would serve no purpose. In the book of Isaiah, as we proceed, we will find several examples of important historical events which are easily identified. Names are named, and detail is supplied. It is helpful for us to be aware that different interpretations of the catastrophe are current.

Sacrifice and Ritual

Addressing the princes and leaders of Jerusalem as ". . . you rulers of Sodom," the author brings to us a speech by Yahweh expressing his extreme displeasure with sacrificial worship:

> What to me is the multitude of your sacrifices?
>   says the LORD.
> I have had enough of burnt offerings of rams
>   and the fat of fed beasts;
> I do not delight in the blood of bulls,

> or of lambs or of goats.
> When you come to appear before me,
>   who asked this from your hand?
> Trample my courts no more; bringing offerings is futile;
>   incense is an abomination to me.
> New moon and sabbath and calling of convocation—
>   I cannot endure solemn assemblies with iniquity.
> Your new moon and your appointed feasts my soul hates;
>   they have become a burden to me.
>   I have become weary of bearing them.
> When you stretch out your hands, I will hide my eyes from you;
>   even though you make many prayers I will not listen;
>   your hands are full of blood.
> Wash yourselves; make yourselves clean;
>   remove the evil of your doings from before my eyes;
> cease to do evil, learn to do good;
>   seek justice, rescue the oppressed.
>   defend the orphan, plead for the widow (Is 1:11–17).

This speech by Yahweh has a parallel in the book of Amos (5:21–24). Both speeches are the words of the Lord in which he expresses his displeasure with their festivals and assemblies and the sacrifices of their fatted beasts. Both speeches end with an admonition to do that which is more important, that is, to live a righteous and just life.

In Isaiah it is the many prayers of the festive occasions to which Yahweh will not listen; in Amos it is the "melody of your harps." Isaiah mentions that their incense, used in the ceremonies to disguise the odors of sacrificed animals, is an abomination to him.[12]

What does the passage mean? Commentators have had trouble taking this oracle of Yahweh at face value. Most scholars soften its harshness by saying something like this: This passage does not condemn sacrificial worship *per se*.

It will assist us in interpretation if we can identify its source. How do we account for these two passages so similar in content and form? There are many possibilities. Could one of the prophets have copied from the other? Could both prophets have produced similar output because of similar feelings and viewpoint? These two proposals are highly unlikely, and there is a better explanation. The following passage from Jeremiah, written almost a hundred years after the ministry of Isaiah, is more likely to hold the key:

> For in the day that I brought your ancestors out of the land of
> Egypt, I did not speak to them or command them concerning

burnt offerings and sacrifices. But this command I gave them. "Obey my voice, and I will be your God, and you shall be my people; and walk only in the way that I command you, so that it may be well with you" (Jer 7:22–23).

Jeremiah used the language of Deuteronomy to attack the torah of the Aaronid priesthood. The phrase, "so that it may be well for you," is a repeated Deuteronomic expression.

During the days of Josiah and the last decade of the seventh century, there were in fact two competing priesthoods and two competing torahs (collections of laws).[13] The torah of the Deuteronomists was the core of the book of Deuteronomy, chapters 12 through 26, which did not include the same kind of detailed instructions for sacrifices, offerings, and priestly procedures found in the priestly writings. The torah of the Aaronid priesthood was the torah which now appears in the books of Leviticus and Numbers. This was the torah

> . . . of burnt offerings, the grain offering, the sin offering, the guilt offering, the offering of ordination, and the sacrifice of well-being (Lev 7:37).

The bottom line here is this. It was the circle of Deuteronomistic scribes which valued the oracles of the eighth century prophets, and it was this circle which redacted their oracles. The two magnificent passages which we have been discussing, the one in Amos beginning with "I hate I despise your festivals," and the one in Isaiah beginning with the words "What to me is the multitude of your sacrifices? says the LORD," find their home in the latter days of Judah's existence, the seventh century, not in the earlier century of Isaiah and Amos. For this reason we believe they are the work of a Josianic redactor. Let us not try to reduce their harshness. Whoever placed them in their present location had strong feelings. He would probably be surprised to read comments by many present day scholars that he did not condemn sacrificial worship *per se*.

These two passages are in complete harmony with the heart of Psalm 51:

> For you have no delight in sacrifice:
> If I were to give a burnt offering,
>   you would not be pleased.

PARALLELS BETWEEN THE BOOK OF AMOS AND ISAIAH 1–5		
Subject	**Amos**	**Isaiah**
Oppression and abuse of the poor	2:6–7; 5:11; 8:6	3:15
Words against the women of the capital cities	4:1–3	3:16–24
Against drunkenness	4:1; 6:6	5:11, 22
Empty houses	5:11	5:9
The day of the Lord	5:18–20	2:11ff
Corrupt administration of justice (bribes)	5:12	1:23; 10:1–2
Critical comments about instruments of music	6:5; 5:23	5:12
The Lord's displeasure with sacrificial offerings	5:21–23	1:13–15

The sacrifice acceptable to God is a broken spirit:
a broken and a contrite heart,[14] O God, you will not despise
(Ps 51:16–17).

Comparing these two passages, one in Isaiah and the other in Amos, brings us to a point where we can note other parallels between the book of Amos and the first five chapters of the book of Isaiah.[15]

Values of the Past

There seems to be a theme underlying the oracles of the eighth century prophets which looks to the past as a more perfect time. In Hosea it was Israel's youth which was cited:

When Israel was a child, I loved him . . .
it was I who taught Ephraim to walk (Hos 11:1,3a).

In Amos it was the passing of the old values which caused the farmers of Israel to suffer at the hands of the powerful urban elite. Now in Isaiah we find that he too looked to the past as a better time. He speaks of Jerusalem:

> How the faithful city
>   has become a whore!
> Righteousness lodged in her—
>   but now murderers! (1:21).

And later—

And I will restore your judges as at the first, and your counselors as at the beginning (1:26).

When was this idealized time in the past of which Isaiah speaks? Isaiah was not referring to the period of the judges. For Isaiah "the beginning" would more likely be the days when Jerusalem first became the capital of Israel, the reign of David. In the Deuteronomistic History kings were often compared with David.

Hezekiah . . . was twenty-five years old when he began to reign; he reigned twenty-nine years in Jerusalem. . . . He did what was right in the sight of the LORD, just as his ancestor David had done (2 Kgs 18:2–3).

As the prologue comes to an end we are introduced to one of the main differences between Isaiah and the other three eighth century prophets, namely the importance for Isaiah of the role to be played in God's plan for the future by the house of David.

STUDY QUESTIONS

1. Why do we call chapter 1 of Isaiah a prologue?

2. The opening paragraphs of a book of the Hebrew Bible are often identified as being later than the material which follows in the body of the book. Give some examples.

3. What is the accusation which appears in the opening verses?

4. To what class were most of the oracles of the eighth century prophets addressed?

5. A catastrophe is referred to, and described, in verses 5–9. Read these verses. Name three possible events which could be referred to in these verses.

6. Why did Isaiah refer to God as the Holy One of Israel, rather than the Holy One of Judah?

7. During the seventh century, one hundred years after Isaiah's activity, a circle of scribes expanded the oracles of Isaiah. What was the name of this school, and what constituted their torah?

8. Give examples of how the eighth century prophets looked to the values of Israel's past.

NOTES

1. See Gerhard von Rad, *Deuteronomy: A Commentary* (Philadelphia: Westminster Press, 1975), p. 12. Also, when we refer to the canonical version of a book of the Bible, we are referring to the final version of the scroll as accepted by the church, the version which appears in our Bible today.

2. Robert Wilson in his book *Prophecy and Society in Ancient Israel* (Philadelphia: Westminster, 1984), p. 261, observes that books of the prophets in the Judean tradition have title verses stating that the prophet *saw* the oracles or the words contained in the book. For example, in Micah 1:1 we read "The word of the LORD that came to Micah . . . which he saw concerning Samaria and Jerusalem." The title of Habakkuk reads, "The oracle that the prophet Habakkuk saw." Wilson distinguishes between prophets of the Judean tradition and prophets of the Ephraimitic tradition. He considers Hosea and Jeremiah as Ephraimitic prophets. For his discussion of Hebrew words for prophet, including *Hazeh*, and *nabi*, see his chapter 5.

3. The title, "Holy One of Israel," appears at least twenty-seven times in the book of Isaiah, and only a few times in the rest of the Hebrew Bible. It appears twice in Jeremiah, 50:29, and 51:5. No similar title appears in the original oracles of the other three eighth century prophets.

4. In the fourth chapter of Amos there is a liturgy of judgment

where five forms of catastrophic judgments are mentioned in Israel's past, each one ending with the response *Yet you did not return to me, says the LORD.* After the statement of the five judgments, the paragraph appears containing the famous words, "Therefore . . . prepare to meet your God, O Israel."

5. John H. Hayes and Stuart A. Irvine, *Isaiah, the Eighth Century Prophet* (Nashville: Abingdon, 1987), pp. 69–70 and 83–84.

6. See John H. Hayes and Paul K. Hooker, *A New Chronology for the Kings of Israel and Judah* (Atlanta: John Knox Press, 1988), p. 55.

7. See pages 72 and 73 of *Isaiah, the Eighth Century Prophet,* cited above by Hayes and Irvine.

8. R.E. Clements, *The New Century Bible Commentary 1–39* (Grand Rapids: Eerdmans, 1987), pp. 30–32.

9. Consult the chart on p. 328 of the text by Lawrence Boadt, *Reading the Old Testament: An Introduction* (Mahwah: Paulist Press, 1984).

10. See section 15 by Joseph Jensen, O.S.B. and William H. Irwin, C.S.B., "Isaiah 1–39," *The New Jerome Bible Commentary* (Englewood Cliffs: Prentice-Hall, 1990), p. 231.

11. Otto Kaiser, *Isaiah 1–12* (Philadelphia: Westminster, 1983), p. 20.

12. Gale Yee in her book *Composition and Tradition in the Book of Hosea* (Atlanta: Scholars Press, 1987), points out that burning incense is singled out in the Deuteronomistic History as being associated with the sin of Jeroboam. She cites 1 Kings 13:2 and 2 Kings 23:5. We should also notice the similarity of language in the Isaiah speech (1:11–17), and the words of a Josianic redactor in chapter 2 of Hosea where the fate of Israel is described: "I will put an end to all her mirth, her festivals, her new moons, her sabbaths, and all her appointed festivals" (v. 11).

13. For a discussion of the two priesthoods, the Levites and the Aaronids, and the two competing torahs, see Richard Elliott Friedman's book, *The Exile and Biblical Narrative* (Chico: Scholars Press, 1981), pp. 74–77.

14. The Hebrew word for heart, *leb,* is a key word in Deuteronomy. It appears once in Leviticus, once in Numbers, and forty-five times in Deuteronomy. For the Deuteronomist, religion was a matter

of the heart. This is one of the characteristics which distinguished the Deuteronomists from the Aaronids.

15. We have elected not to discuss the parallels in this text. The verses can be looked up. Here are several of them. Under the heading "empty houses," in Amos 5:11 we read, "You have built houses of hewn stone, but you will not live in them." In Isaiah 5:9 we read, ". . . many houses shall be desolate, large and beautiful houses, without inhabitant." Also, under the heading "critical comments about instruments of music," both Amos and Isaiah mention the playing of musical instruments associated with drinking parties. Amos 6:5 reads, ". . . who sing idle songs to the sound of the harp, and like David improvise on instruments of music." In Isaiah 5:12 we read, ". . . whose feasts consist of lyre and harp, tambourine and flute and wine."

Chapter 3

THE DOMINATION OF THE NEAR EAST BY ASSYRIA

Suggested Scripture Readings:

Isaiah 7
2 Kings 16

The background for understanding many of the oracles of Isaiah is provided by the terrifying military threat posed by Assyria against Judah and the small nations of the Palestine–Syria area during the period of Isaiah's public ministry. Nations threatened with invasion and destruction by the mighty Assyrian military machine included Judah, Israel, Syria, Philistia, Moab, Ammon and Phoenicia. Even Egypt and Ethiopia were vulnerable to Assyrian domination.

Assyria was an ancient power which took its name from a powerful city-state named Asshur, located on the east side of the fertile crescent, north of Babylon, on the Tigris River. Asshur was the ancient name of a city-state and it was also the name of its chief god. The name Asshur was used in the name adopted by several Assyrian kings including Ashur-dan, Ashur-nasir-pal, and the famous Ashur-bani-pal. Assyria's capital cities included Asshur, Nineveh, and Calnah (Nimrud), all on the Tigris River.

While Assyria dominated the entire Near East for three hundred years, approximately from 900 to 600 B.C.E., to become the first in a series of military powers to "conquer the world" (Assyria, Babylon, Persia, Greece, Rome), it was in the days of Isaiah that Assyria, under the leadership of Tiglath-pileser (744–727), renewed its aggression and strengthened its military domination of the Mediterranean na-

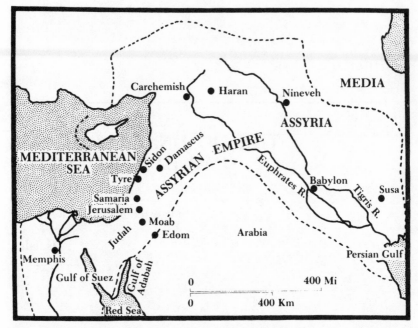

The Assyrian Empire in the 8th and 7th Centuries B.C.

tions. Tiglath-pileser III decided that Assyria was going to be a world empire with him as its emperor. His seizing the throne of Babylon and declaring himself King Pulu was just one step in his ambitious plan.

To increase the wealth of Assyria he planned to control the trade routes through Palestine–Syria and the seaports of the eastern Mediterranean. He also planned to subdue the small nations and enrich the Assyrian treasury with tribute from all of them.

Assyrian Characteristics in the Days of Isaiah

Under Tiglath-pileser and his immediate successors Assyria developed and strengthened characteristics which can be viewed under seven headings.

(1) Values of Military Aggression

The primary societal values of Assyria were military values. The nation's chief energies were put into expansion involving the subjection of other nations. Not only were her neighbors prey, but distant nations were prime targets for this culture of war.

(2) Organization Skills

Assyrian military leaders were able to accomplish their victories by regimenting and moving large groups of soldiers, demonstrating coordination and communication skills. Along with these skills the latest in military weaponry was developed for destroying walled cities.

(3) Provincial System

Turning an independent nation into a province while allowing an indigenous king to rule for Assyria was perfected by Tiglath-pileser. In the *Cambridge Ancient History*, the author of the volume on Assyria states: ". . . the system of annexation and provincial government so thoroughly carried out over western Asia distinguished the Assyrian domination in its character from any previously exercised by Babylonians, Hittites, or Egyptians."

(4) Vassal Treaty Administration

Assyria revived an ancient form of Hittite vassal treaty. In the vassal treaty there were two parties, the mighty and the weak (the vassal). The vassal nation would receive protection from the mighty party in return for obedience and tribute (taxation).

(5) Use of Severe Cruelty

Assyrian kings bragged about their cruelty. They wrote about impaling, beheading, and flaying their enemies and commissioned monuments depicting these acts of cruelty. The purpose of acts of cruelty was to paralyze their enemies with fear.

(6) Relocation of Defeated Populations

It was Tiglath-pileser III who perfected the practice of relocating entire populations of city-states and capital cities on which the entire nation was dependent. For purposes of control, western populations were moved east, and eastern populations were moved to the west. Relocation was implemented when the vassal treaty relationship was unworkable.

(7) Fondness for Monuments Boasting of Great Victories

Assyrians enjoyed the practice of recording in permanent monuments details of their military victories. These records have been found on pavement slabs, monoliths, prisms, walls, and gates. Reliefs of marvelous detail have been found recreating battle scenes and celebrating Assyrian conquests.

Assyria and Israel/Judah

About the time that King Uzziah (739) died and Isaiah had his vision of Yahweh in the temple, the Assyrians had already returned to Palestine in strength. The Bible history informs us that Menahem (745–738), king of Israel, had to pay a large amount of tribute to Assyria to hold on to his throne.[1]

> King Pul of Assyria came against the land: Menahem gave Pul a thousand talents of silver, so that he might help him confirm his hold on the royal power. Menahem exacted the money from Israel, that is, from all the wealthy, fifty shekels of silver from each one, to give to the king of Assyria (2 Kgs 15:19–20).

This was a tremendous hardship on the economy of Israel. Historians have estimated that sixty thousand people had to take part in this taxation if it is accurately recorded. There was bitterness against Menahem, and two years following his death, Pekah, an Israelite captain, with a history of power grabbing attempts, assassinated Menahem's son, Pekahiah (737), and seized the throne of Israel.

In the meantime, Rezin, king of Syria in Damascus, took the leadership role in the formation of an anti-Assyrian coalition. A century earlier a similar coalition which included Ahab of Israel (874–853) and the king of Syria had met Shalmaneser III in a massive battle at Karkar (853).

Pekah of Israel was part of this new coalition, and Ahaz of Judah was expected to follow suit. When Ahaz made known his intention to remain neutral and not support the anti-Assyrian coalition, Rezin and Pekah planned to attack the city of Jerusalem and replace Ahaz with a foreign king identified as the son of Tabeel.

> King Rezin of Aram and King Pekah . . . of Israel went up to attack Jerusalem. . . . When the house of David heard that Aram had allied itself with Ephraim, the heart of Ahaz and

KINGS OF ASSYRIA DURING MINISTRY OF ISAIAH		
Name	Dates	Information
Tiglath-Pileser III	744–727	Under his leadership Assyrian domination of Syria-Palestine was strengthened. He marched west to destroy the Syrian-Israelite coalition. He received tribute from Ahaz and Menahem. He also took Babylon.
Shalmanesser V	726–722	When Hoshea stopped paying heavy tribute to Assyria, Shalmanesser came against Israel and took Hoshea prisoner. Samaria was under siege for three years.
Sargon II	722–705	He finished the capture of Samaria and the final relocation of the Israelites. Captives from the east were brought to repopulate Israel.
Sennacherib	704–681	He destroyed forty-six towns and fortresses in Judah and threatened Jerusalem. Jerusalem was not captured and Hezekiah was allowed to continue on the throne.

the heart of his people shook as the trees of the forest shake before the wind (Is 7:1–2).

In 734 Tiglath-pileser marched against the coalition, first capturing the coastal areas of Philistia and Gaza to prevent interference from Egypt. He later captured Damascus and killed Rezin. In the Deuteronomistic History, which was compiled a century after these events, it is stated that Tiglath-pileser came against the coalition in response to a request of Ahaz (2 Kgs 16:7). In a recent book on Isaiah this fact is challenged as highly unlikely. The Bible history also reports that Ahaz of Judah went to Damascus to meet Tiglath-pileser and that Ahaz paid tribute to Assyria. There is no reason to doubt this. It is also reported in Assyrian records that tribute was received at this time from Edom, Moab, Ammon, Askelon, and Gaza.[2]

Along with Damascus, Tiglath-pileser is reported to have taken Galilee and the land of Naphtali, areas which at one time had belonged to Israel, but more recently had been under Syrian control. For reasons not clear, Pekah was allowed to continue to reign in Samaria until he was killed by Hoshea, the last king of Israel (732–722). Under Shalmaneser V, Hoshea became a vassal of Assyria, but in 725 he conspired with Egypt to throw off the Assyrian yoke. Shalmaneser marched against Samaria and made Hoshea a prisoner for three years. In 722 Samaria was destroyed and the inhabitants carried away into Assyrian captivity never to return. The northern kingdom of Israel was finished. Because of the death of Shalmaneser, Sargon II is said to have completed the resettling of the Israelites.

Sargon II (722–705), sometime after 720, was able to establish trading relationships with northern Egypt. Cooperation between Egyptians and Assyrians is referred to in an oracle of Isaiah (chapter 19). The reign of Sargon was filled with revolt, and Sargon was busy running from one troubled area to another. He marched against Ashdod, Armenia, Media, Babylon, and Anatolia. It was during his reign that Merodach-baladan became king of the city-state of Babylon.

> At that time King Merodach-baladan son of Baladan of Babylonia sent envoys with letters and a present to Hezekiah, for he heard that he had been sick and had recovered (Is 39:1).

In 705, leading Assyrian soldiers against Anatolia, Sargon II was killed in battle. It was a time of rebellion against Assyria and of hope that Assyrian power was over. Hezekiah was a participant in the general revolt.

Assyrian aggression was not over, however. Four years later Sennacherib came west:

> In the fourteenth year of King Hezekiah, King Sennacherib of Assyria came against all the fortified cities of Judah and captured them (Is 36:1).

The high point of this invasion was the destruction of the walled city of Lachish, the details of which are preserved for us in a massive relief of tremendous detail, reconstructed today in the British museum. Sennacherib did horrible damage to the countryside of Judah, but his siege of Jerusalem ended abruptly without victory. As the prophetic ministry of Isaiah came to an end, we read this about Sennacherib:

> Then King Sennacherib of Assyria left, went home, and lived in Ninevah. As he was worshiping in the house of his god Nisroch, his sons . . . killed him with the sword, and they escaped into the land of Ararat (Is 37:37–38).

Assyria continued as a world power for another century after the end of the eighth century. In the middle of the seventh century Ashurbanipal invaded Egypt and captured the great temple city of Thebes. Assyria controlled the fertile crescent from the Euphrates to the Nile. By the end of the seventh century, however, Assyria had collapsed from its own weight. "By 609, the Assyrian nation was no more, fallen to a coalition of Babylonians and Medes."[3]

STUDY QUESTIONS

1. Why was it important for Assyria to control the Palestine–Syria area?

2. Before resorting to mass resettlement of a particular population, what type of political control did Assyria implement?

3. Explain the term *vassal treaty*.

4. In addition to the Hebrew scriptures, what are our sources for the Assyrian invasions and conquests? Give several examples.

5. Discuss the anti-Assyrian coalition headed by Rezin, king of Syria, in the eighth century. What did Tiglath-pileser do about the coalition?

6. Explain the details leading up to the final destruction of Samaria (and Israel) during the reign of Hoshea. What is the theological explanation of the fall of Israel? (Read 2 Kings 17:7–18.)

MAJOR EVENTS OF ASSYRIAN INTERACTION WITH ISRAEL/JUDAH

Information	Date	Reference
Menahem of Israel paid large tribute to Pul (Tiglath-pileser) to confirm his hold on the throne of Israel.	745–738	2 Kings 15:19
Pekah reigned in Israel, participating in an anti-Assyrian coalition. With Rezin, he came against and threatened Ahaz and Jerusalem.	734	2 Kings 16:5 Isaiah 7:1
Tiglath-pileser defeated Damascus and subdued Israel. He provincialized the Palestinian coast, Syria, and Galilee.	733	2 Kings 15:29
Ahaz paid tribute to Tiglath-pileser.	733	2 Kings 16:8
Ahaz went to Damascus to meet Tiglath-pileser.	733	2 Kings 16:10
Hoshea killed Pekah and took the throne of Israel as a vassal of Assyria. He paid tribute to Shalmaneser V.	732	2 Kings 15:30 2 Kings 17:3
Shalmaneser imprisoned Hoshea when Hoshea conspired with Egypt and neglected to pay tribute.	725	2 Kings 17:4
Samaria was captured and Israel was destroyed by Shalmaneser V.	722	2 Kings 17:6 2 Kings 18:9
Sargon II completed the provincialization of Israel and the carrying away of the population.	722/1	2 Kings 17:6 2 Kings 17:24
Sargon was killed leading Assyrian soldiers in Anatolia. There was hope throughout the east that Assyrian power would fade.	705	Isaiah 24:14–16a
Four years later Sennacherib invaded the west and destroyed Lachish and many cities of Judah. He also threatened Jerusalem. He received heavy tribute from Hezekiah.	701	2 Kings 18:13 Isaiah 36:1 2 Kings 18:16
Sennacherib withdrew from Judah.	701	Isaiah 37:37
Sennacherib was murdered in Nineveh by his sons. Esarhaddon succeeded him.	681	Isaiah 37:38

NOTES

1. Menahem was not the first king of Israel to pay tribute to an Assyrian king. Jehu (841–814) is pictured in a panel of the famous Black Obelisk of Shalmaneser III bowing at the feet of the Assyrian king while his attendants present gifts.

2. *ANET*, 282–284.

3. Lawrence Boadt, *Reading the Old Testament*, p. 44.

Chapter 4

EARLY ORACLES

Suggested Scripture Reading:

Isaiah 2–5

In this chapter we will discuss some of the oracles appearing between the second title verse of Isaiah (2:1) and the vision of Isaiah in the temple (chapter 6). Here is an outline of these chapters:

2:2-5	The glorious future of Zion
2:6–22	Judgment on the proud
3:1–12	Disintegration of society
3:13–15	Abuse of the poor
3:16–4:1	Judgment on the women of Judah
4:2–6	Preservation of a remnant
5:1–7	Allegory of the vineyard
5:8–24	Injustice denounced and punished
	The first six of seven woes.
5:25–30	A foreign invasion described

If an earlier scroll of Isaiah started with chapter 2, verse 1 as we have suggested,[1]

The word that Isaiah son of Amoz saw concerning Judah and Jerusalem (2:1),

then this early collection of the oracles had an optimistic opening. An idealized future for Zion is visualized:

In days to come the mountain of the Lord's house shall be established as the highest of the mountains, and shall be raised above the hills; all the nations shall stream to it (2:2).

The name Zion (v. 3) is used interchangeably with Jerusalem (v. 3), the mountain of the Lord's house (v. 2), the mountain of the Lord (v. 3), and the house of the God of Jacob (v. 3). Ancient Israel lived in a pre-scientific age where height and apparent nearness to the clouds and the sky had theological significance.

At the conclusion of this hopeful oracle we are told that the people

. . . shall beat their swords into plowshares,
   and spears into pruning hooks;
nation shall not lift up sword against nation,
   neither shall they learn war any more (2:4).

This same inspiring oracle appears in Micah, word for word, with the addition of an idealistic, rural conclusion:

. . . but they shall all sit under their own vines
   and under their own fig trees
   and no one shall make them afraid;
for the mouth of the Lord of Hosts has spoken (Mi 4:4).

The amount of scholarship devoted to the origin of this oracle has been voluminous. Did Isaiah copy from Micah? Did Micah copy from Isaiah? Did both prophets quote an old confession? Or is the passage a later addition to both books?[2]

There is a Zion Psalm which ends with the destruction of weapons of war:

He makes wars to cease to the end of the earth;
   he breaks the bow, and shatters the spear;
   he burns the shields with fire (Ps 46:9).

However in this Psalm it is God who destroys the weapons; in the Isaiah passage the people destroy the weapons of war. In the Isaiah pericope the triumph of peace seems to originate with a changed human nature:

Nation shall not lift up sword against nation,
    neither shall they learn war any more (2:4).

This splendid, concrete statement of universal hope is timeless. If we cannot identify the exact time of its origin, we can still feel the power and lift of its inspiration.

Judgment on the Proud

There are nine oracles found in chapters 2 through 5, and all of them, except for the first (the glorious future of Zion) and the sixth (preservation of a remnant), are filled with bad news. The prophet strikes out against the pride of the elders and the princes who have misled the people and robbed from the poor:

The LORD enters into judgment
    with the elders and princes of his people:
It is you who have devoured the vineyard;
    the spoil of the poor is in your houses.
What do you mean by crushing my people,
    by grinding the face of the poor?
    says the LORD God of hosts (3:14–15).

Isaiah, like the other eighth century prophets, was a stern messenger of doom. These prophets were extremely critical of the society of the ruling classes, and with Isaiah we discover a particular attack on human pride. In this passage a variety of symbols for pride is poetically employed. As you read it, notice how the symbols appear in a *list*. This is typical of Isaiah:

For the LORD of hosts has a day
    against all that is proud and lofty,
    against all that is lifted up and high;
    against all the cedars of Lebanon, lofty and lifted up;
    against all the oaks of Bashan;
    against all the high mountains,

against all the lofty hills;
against every high tower,
against every fortified wall;
against all the ships of Tarshish,
against all the beautiful craft.
The haughtiness of people shall be humbled,
and the pride of everyone shall be brought low;
and the LORD alone will be exalted on that day (2:12–17).

As we compile our own list of the characteristics of Isaiah's oracles, we will include his particular attack on human pride.

The Wives of the Ruling Class

In most societies, women enliven and enrich the scene of human activity by adorning themselves with beautiful, decorous accessories which go beyond the basic functionality of clothing. Ancient Jerusalem was no different. Like Amos, Isaiah attacked the wives of the ruling classes. In doing so, Isaiah (or a redactor) has given us a list which has added fine detail to our picture of daily life in ancient Judah:

—anklets
—headbands
—crescents
—pendants
—bracelets
—scarfs
—headdresses
—armlets
—sashes
—perfume boxes
—amulets
—festal robes
—mantles
—garments of gauze
—linen garments
—turbans
—veils

The tragic dimension of this is that the women of ancient society were always among the obvious victims of warfare. Ancient capital cities, including Jerusalem, were called *daughter* and *mother*, and each woman of Jerusalem was a symbol of the vulnerability of *daughter Zion* (1:8).

The Vineyard

My beloved had a vineyard on a very fertile hill.
He dug it and cleared it of stones,
   and planted it with choice vines;
he built a watchtower in the midst of it,
   and hewed out a wine vat in it;
he expected it to yield grapes,
   but it yielded wild grapes (5:1–2).

Building a vineyard involved a great amount of work and continued care. The land had to be cleared and dug, the seeds planted, the vines cultivated (hoed), the walls built and kept in repair to keep farm animals out. A watchtower was a necessity. A winepress had to be built and the grapes harvested, pressed and stored. In this allegory, the owner did everything right, but the outcome was only "wild grapes," small, hard, bitter. The figure from viniculture also appears in the Psalms:

You brought a vine out of Egypt;
   you drove out the nations and planted it.
You cleared the ground for it;
   it took deep root and filled the land (Ps 80:8–9).

In the Psalm, the vineyard flourishes. In Isaiah, the vineyard is only a disappointment for the owner. For this reason he will remove its hedge and break down its wall. We know that the owner is God, because only God controls the rain:

I will also command the clouds
   that they rain no rain upon it (5:6).

Instead of producing large, juice-filled grapes, the area will be overrun with "briers and thorns." *Briers and thorns* is a descriptive phrase which appears several places in Isaiah.

The listener (reader) is provided with an explanation:

For the vineyard of the LORD of hosts
  is the house of Israel,
  and the people of Judah are his pleasant planting;
He expected justice, but saw bloodshed;
  righteousness, but heard a cry (5:7)!

The closing sentence serves to introduce a series of seven *woes* condemning the behavior of certain Judeans who have offended and provoked the Lord of hosts and the Holy One of Israel. It is possible then that the purpose of the song of the vineyard was to introduce a theological explanation of calamities which had befallen Israel in the north, and were also threatening Judah. During the reign of Menahem in Samaria (745–732), at least three calamities befell the northern kingdom:

(1) Israel's territory was reduced by her immediate neighbors allowing Menahem to control only the central hill country.

. . . the Arameans on the east and the Philistines on the west,
. . . devoured Israel with open mouth (Is 9:12).

At this time Uzziah was still alive and Jotham was a co-regent in Jerusalem.

(2) As we have already reported, Menahem was forced to pay heavy tribute to Tiglath-pileser to maintain his throne, harming the economy of Israel.

Menahem gave Pul a thousand talents of silver, so that he might help him confirm his hold on the royal power. Menahem exacted the money from Israel, that is, from all the wealthy, fifty shekels of silver from each one, to give to the king of Assyria (2 Kgs 15:19–20).

(3) The earthquake took place sometime during, or shortly before, the reign of Menahem. It is referred to in the woe section introduced by the song of the vineyard.

Sheol has enlarged its appetite and opened its mouth beyond
    measure;
the nobility of Jerusalem and her multitude go down, her
    throng and all who exult in her.
. . . the anger of the LORD was kindled against his people,
and he stretched out his hand against them and struck them;

the mountains quaked, and their corpses were like refuse in the
streets (Is 5:14, 25).

Although the song of the vineyard is sung to the inhabitants of Jerusalem (5:3), the source of the disappointment could primarily be the
northern kingdom Israel (7:1a). If this were so, then these words
would apply to the destruction of Samaria:

I will remove its hedge, and it shall be devoured;
    I will break down its wall, and it shall be trampled down.
I will make it a waste;
    it shall not be pruned or hoed,
    and briers and thorns shall grow up (5:5–6).

During the lifetime of Isaiah, Samaria was destroyed. Jerusalem was
not. However, the point of the vineyard story is that the owner of the
vineyard cannot be blamed for the wild grapes. He did everything
correctly. Judah and Israel cannot blame God for the troubles which
have come to them.

The story of the vineyard introduces seven *woe* statements. Six of
the *woe* statements are in 5:8–23, and the seventh is found after the
memoirs of Isaiah (6–8:18) in 10:1–4.[3] Some scholars have identified
the woe statements as funeral laments. The content is not that of a
lament however. These statements are probably based on a primitive
incantation or curse form.[4] The woe statements provide detail concerning why Israel and Judah deserve punishment from the hand of
God. Some of the woes have been extended by the addition of editorial comments.

THE SEVEN WOE STATEMENTS[5]

1. Woe to those who join house to house, who add field to field.
2. Woe to those who rise early in the morning, that they may run
   after strong drink.
3. Woe to those who draw iniquity with cords of falsehood, who
   draw sin as with cart ropes.
4. Woe to those who call evil good and good evil.
5. Woe to those who are wise in their own eyes.
6. Woe to those who are heroes at drinking wine.
7. Woe to those who decree iniquitous decrees, and the writers who
   keep writing oppression.

Various themes of societal injustice run through the *woes*, including public drunkenness and idleness (2), self-satisfaction and pride (5), rationalization concerning society's structural problems (4), and the production of decrees to promote the oppression of the rural poor by the elite of Jerusalem (7). But the jewel of the woe statements is the first, which is a masterpiece of brevity.

> Woe to those who join house to house,
>   who add field to field,
> until there is no more room,
>   and you are made to dwell alone
>   in the midst of the land (5:8).

In these few words Isaiah has vividly pictured the most outrageous social problem facing eighth century Israel/Judah. This was the growth of large estates, created by seizing plots of land from farming families in times of hardship, turning small independent farmers into debt slaves. If these poor, rural families were lucky, they became tenant farmers on land which had belonged to their families for generations. In some cases they were simply forced off the land by rich owners who wanted spaciousness for their own comfort and privacy. Not only did the elite end up owning the land, but they also owned the peasants, who were forever in debt, supported both by corrupt laws, and by the corrupt administration of just laws.[6]

The Terror of an Approaching Army

The collection of early oracles ends with an ancient marvel of poetic description. An enemy army moves forward with a precision which can only produce terror. As you read it you can smell the fear, and hear the sound of the horses' hooves. Against this determined invader, Judah, without the salvation of the Lord, would have no hope:

> . . . lo, swiftly, speedily it comes!
> None is weary, none stumbles,
>   none slumbers or sleeps,
> not a waistcloth is loose,
>   not a sandal-thong broken;
> their arrows are sharp,
>   all their bows bent,

their horses' hoofs seem like flint,
  and their wheels like the whirlwind.
Their roaring is like a lion
  like young lions they roar;
they growl and seize their prey,
  they carry it off, and none can rescue.
They will growl over it on that day,
  like the roaring of the sea (5:26–30).

STUDY QUESTIONS

1. In the story of the vineyard, why was the owner disappointed? What is the identity of the vineyard?

2. Name three calamities which befell the northern kingdom, Israel, during the early ministry of Isaiah.

3. Explain the severe social significance of the woe which condemns those who join ". . . house to house, who add field to field."

4. Why did Amos and Isaiah condemn the lifestyle of the wives of the elite of Samaria and Jerusalem?

5. A famous oracle appears, word for word, both in Micah and Isaiah. Identify this oracle and give three possible explanations for this.

6. There are two title verses in the first two chapters of Isaiah, 1:1 and 2:1. What could this mean?

NOTES

1. Many scholars think that Isaiah 2:1 was not a title, but an early scholarly insertion (a marginal note), meant to identify Isaiah as the author, rather than Micah, of the famous quotation which follows concerning the beating of swords into plowshares. See for example Peter R. Ackroyd's article "The Book of Isaiah" (*The Interpreter's One-Volume Commentary on the Bible*, Nashville: Abingdon, 1971), p. 333. In this case, this paragraph would not have been the first paragraph of an ancient scroll, but the last paragraph of the prologue which we have discussed in our chapters 3 and 4.

2. Otto Kaiser, in *Isaiah 1–12* (Philadelphia: Westminster, 1981),

has a list of mostly German scholars who have written on several sides of the question (p. 52). Kaiser's view ends inconclusively and depends, he says, on the age of Zion theology. John Hayes, *op. cit.*, sees both prophets, Micah and Isaiah, "using an older text."

3. The seventh "woe" statement is separated from the sixth "woe" statement by the memoirs of Isaiah (6:1–9:7). It is called the "memoirs" because of the use of the first person in chapter 6 and chapter 8. Some commentators prefer to use the German word *Denkschrift* for this section (6:1–9:7). There are some who believe that the memoirs may form the original core of the book of Isaiah. R.E. Clements in his commentary, *Isaiah 1–39*, suggests that the first six woes should be after the memoirs, together with the seventh in chapter 10 (p. 60).

4. Otto Kaiser says the woe form is related to a lament for the dead (*Isaiah 1–12*), p. 96. R.E. Clements (*Isaiah 1–39*) sees the form as an established form of prophetic threat.

5. The "woe" statements are presented here as they appear in the RSV, 1952 translation.

6. Consult Robert Coote's book *Amos Among the Prophets* (Philadelphia: Fortress Press, 1981), pp. 26–36. The serious student of this subject is referred to a paper by Marvin L. Chaney, "Latifundialization and Prophetic Diction in Eighth-Century Israel and Judah." This paper was presented to the SBL/ASOR Sociology of the Monarchy Seminar, Anaheim, California, 1985.

Chapter 5

THE MEMOIRS OF ISAIAH

Suggested Scripture Reading:

Isaiah 6–8:18

In the year that King Uzziah died I saw the LORD sitting upon a throne, high and lifted up; and his train filled the temple (6:1).

The memoirs of Isaiah, beginning with Isaiah's vision in the temple, and extending through the prophetic statement which includes the words:

. . . I and the children whom the LORD has given me are signs and portents in Israel from the LORD of hosts, who dwells on Mount Zion (8:18),

is one of the most exhaustively studied sections of the Hebrew Bible. In an introductory text we could not even hope to summarize the variety of viewpoints available to us on almost every sentence. It is possible, however, to identify the primary issues before us, and to adopt some meaningful approaches.

Was the Vision an Inaugural Prophetic Call?

Scholars have argued both sides of this question. Some have asked why, if this is an initial call to Isaiah, it does not appear at the beginning of the book, like the prophetic calls of Jeremiah and Eze-

40

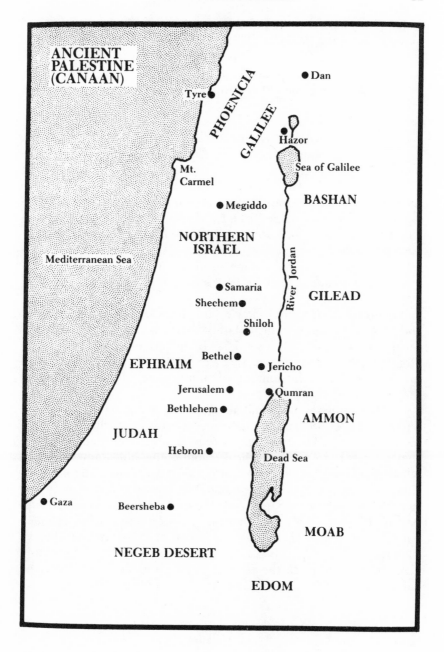

ANCIENT
PALESTINE
(CANAAN)

● Dan

Tyre ●

PHOENICIA

GALILEE

● Hazor

Sea of Galilee

Mt.
Carmel

BASHAN

● Megiddo

NORTHERN
ISRAEL

Mediterranean Sea

River Jordan

● Samaria

Shechem ●

GILEAD

Shiloh
●

Bethel ●

EPHRAIM

● Jericho

Jerusalem ●

● Qumran

Bethlehem ●

AMMON

JUDAH

Hebron ●

Dead Sea

● Gaza

Beersheba ●

MOAB

NEGEB DESERT

EDOM

kiel? In the book of Amos, however, the prophet's call is not referred to until late in the book:

> And the LORD took me from following the flock, and the LORD said to me, "Go prophesy to my people Israel" (Am 7:15).

It is within the realm of possibility that this vision was at the beginning of an independent scroll (The Memoirs of Isaiah), containing the vision and the accounts following of Isaiah's interactions with King Ahaz (Is 6:1–8:18). If this were the case, we might be able to see the seams of its incorporation into a previously existing scroll consisting of a collection of oracles from Isaiah. And indeed we can. There is a liturgical refrain which appears in chapter 5 before the memoirs:

> For all this his anger has not turned away,
> and his hand is stretched out still (5:25),

and reappears four times following the memoirs in 9:12, 9:17, 9:21, and 10:4. We have previously stated that the seventh woe (10:1) was separated from the sixth woe (5:22) by material including the memoirs. These facts are evidence that a collection of oracles was opened for the insertion of the contents of an independent scroll containing the memoirs (6:1–9:7).

If the vision was not an initial call, what else could it have been? It has been suggested that the experience was for the purpose of changing the nature of Isaiah's ministry (which, up to this time, had been similar to that of Amos and Micah), and to give him a new direction which would involve him in major political decisions being made by King Ahaz and, later, King Hezekiah. We have stated previously that the other eighth century prophets did not speak with kings. In support of this view, it is noted that the social criticism of Isaiah which parallels the oracles of Amos (see our chart on this subject in chapter 2) is largely limited to chapters 1 through 5 of Isaiah. The vision in chapter 6 would mark the turning point for Isaiah, separating the nature of his earlier ministry from the rest of his activity.[1]

The Vision

The experience is told to us in the past tense. Considerable time may have passed since the experience. Isaiah did not see God, but a vision of God, compatible with the imagery of his day. The imagery is archaic. Today we would not imagine God as an oversized king sitting on an oversized throne.

Regardless, this picturesque passage completely enthralls the reader. Once we have read it we can't forget it. If this is true, imagine what impact the vision had on Isaiah and how forcefully this experience was lodged in his memory. Elements of temple worship played their part, the smoke of incense, the red coals on the altar, and the antiphonal chants of the seraphs (seraphim), in their places to adore and worship God, to protect his court, and to do his bidding.

We don't know how many seraphs there were, but each had three sets of wings for appropriate uses. With one set they covered their faces from the glory of Yahweh, with another they covered their feet (a euphemism for sexual parts), and with another they flew. They had voices, and they chanted to one another:

Holy, holy, holy is the LORD of hosts;
the whole earth is full of his glory.

Isaiah, in his oracles, would frequently use the title "The Holy One of Israel."[2] Perhaps, for Isaiah, it can be traced back to the impact of this unique experience. The temple began to shake, and Isaiah felt condemned because of his sin and the sin of his people. Before he had a chance to react further, his lips were purified and he was told by a seraph that his guilt had departed and his sin had been blotted out.

Thus purified, Isaiah heard the voice of God saying, "Whom shall I send and who will go for us?" Without hesitation Isaiah replied, "Here am I; send me!"

Isaiah's Commission

At this point in our survey, it would be comfortable to say that Isaiah was told to tell the people of Judah to repent, change their ways, return to the old righteous ways, or face their punishment, but this choice was not presented to them. If we were reading this passage for the first time, we might expect this kind of a message to be ordered by God. But Isaiah's instructions were different:

Go and say to this people:
"Keep listening but do not comprehend;
keep looking but do not understand."

Make the mind of this people dull,
  and stop their ears,
  and shut their eyes,
so that they may not look with their eyes,
  and listen with their ears
and comprehend with their minds,
  and turn and be healed (6:9–10).

Could this mean that punishment was inevitable and there was no escape for the nation whose leaders had turned their back on Yahweh?

This People

To make the words of the commission less harsh, some scholars have suggested that the interpretation of the commission to Isaiah turns on the definition of the words "this people." Recent studies of the eighth century prophets would support this approach. These studies indicate that the original oracles of the eighth century prophets were not addressed to the people of Israel and Judah *en masse*, but to more specific groups of elite decision makers in the capital cities of Samaria and Jerusalem.[3]

Because the vision of Isaiah is closely tied to the interaction between Isaiah and King Ahaz, the meaning of the term "this people" is looked for in this specific activity. Hayes and Irvine in their book *Isaiah The Eighth Century Prophet* identify "this people" as subjects of Ahaz who oppose his neutrality, and who demand that he join the northern kingdom of Israel and Syria in an anti-Assyrian coalition. They are "non-supporters of the Davidic house." It is "this people" whose heart will be hardened as punishment for their rejection of Ahaz, the Davidic king.[4]

The Syro-Ephraimite Coalition

In the days of Ahaz . . . Rezin of Aram and King Pekah, son of Remaliah of Israel, went up to attack Jerusalem. . . . When the house of David heard that Aram [Syria] had allied itself with Ephraim, the heart of Ahaz and the heart of his people shook as the trees of the forest shake before the wind (7:1–2).

DEVELOPMENTS IN THE SYRO-EPHRAIMITIC CRISIS

Dates	Information
738	Tiglath-pileser III had trouble near home with the Uratians, north of Assyria, and was not present in Palestine.
737	Rezin, king of Syria, took the leadership role in an anti-Assyrian coalition. (A century earlier a coalition led by Ahab had driven back an Assyrian army at Qarqar.)
737/6	Pekah, who had seized the throne of Israel by assassination, joined the anti-Assyrian coalition.
735	Because Ahaz refused to join the anti-Assyrian coalition, Rezin and Pekah planned to replace him by force with a foreign king, the son of Tabeel (Is 7:6).
	Rezin assisted the Edomites to take the port of Elath, on the Gulf of Akabah, from Judah (2 Kgs 7:6).
	Ahaz continued refusing to join the coalition, and the prophet Isaiah encouraged Ahaz in this position (Is 7:3–10).
734	Tiglath-pileser came west, killed Rezin, and made Damascus an Assyrian province. Many people were carried into exile.
733/2	Hoshea killed Pekah and became king of a reduced Israel, now called Ephraim (2 Kgs 15:29–30).

Shortly before the death of Uzziah (742),[5] the year of Isaiah's vision, a new Assyrian king by the name of Tiglath-pileser III was able to reorganize Assyria's military strength in the east and set his sights on the Palestine-Syrian area. Israel, the northern kingdom, had experienced several decades of peace from Assyrian invasion before the accession of Tiglath-pileser. The Israelite king Menahem (745–738) was forced to pay heavy tribute to Assyria to hold his throne (2 Kgs 15:19–20). This tribute was so high that the economy of Samaria was threatened. Some scholars believe that the southern kingdom of Judah also related to Assyrian domination through Israel and shared in paying the tribute to Tiglath-pileser.

In 737 an Israelite captain by the name of Pekah was able to assassinate King Pekahiah of Israel and seize the throne with the help of Rezin, king of Syria. These two, Rezin and Pekah, formed the nucleus of an anti-Assyrian coalition, which hoped to repeat the success of a coalition of an earlier century which had been successful in holding back Assyrian advances under Shalmaneser at the battle of Karkara (Qarqar) in 853 B.C.E.

Ahaz of Judah refused to join the anti-Assyrian coalition, so Rezin and Pekah planned to invade Jerusalem and replace him with a foreign king:

> Syria, with Ephraim and the son of Remaliah, has devised evil against you, saying, "Let us go up against Judah and terrify it, and let us conquer it for ourselves, and set up the son of Tabeel as king in the midst of it (Is 7:6).[6]

At the Lord's instruction Isaiah and his son Shear-jashub (a name which means *a remnant shall return*)[7] met with Ahaz ". . . at the end of the conduit of the upper pool on the highway to the fuller's field." Ahaz had gone to this location to inspect an important link in the city's water supply in the event of siege.

Although Ahaz had refused to join the coalition, there were those among his subjects who were not willing to support his decision. It is possible that this group of Judeans even favored the replacement of Ahaz with the son of Tabeel, the plan of Rezin and Pekah referred to above (Is 7:6).

A Threat to the House of David

What is at issue here is the continuation of the house of David on the throne of Jerusalem. In an earlier verse in the account we read:

When the house of David was told, "Syria is in league with Ephraim," his heart and the heart of his people shook as the trees of the forest shake before the storm (Is 7:2).

Also, later, when Isaiah is announcing the birth of a son in connection with a sign from Yahweh, he began his speech with the words, "Hear then, O house of David" (7:12). Some bad things had happened to the house of David. Uzziah had been stricken with leprosy, and this could have been interpreted as a sign of a withdrawal of Yahweh's blessing:

The LORD struck the king, so that he was leprous to the day of his death, and lived in a separate house (2 Kgs 15:5).

Also, at this time, the important seaport of Elath had been wrenched from Judean control.

At that time the king of Edom recovered Elath for Edom and drove the Judeans from Elath (2 Kgs 16:6).

And now there was great pressure on Ahaz to join the anti-Assyrian coalition. This pressure may have come from Judean citizens, even from some advisors of Ahaz. Isaiah, like Hosea, was opposed to foreign alliances of any kind, and considered these alliances as evidence of rejection of Yahweh. When Israel had looked to foreign alliances for salvation, Hosea had written:

Ephraim is like a dove, silly and without sense,
    calling to Egypt, going to Assyria (Hos 7:11).

Israel is swallowed up;
    already they are among the nations as a useless vessel.
For they have gone up to Assyria,
    a wild ass wandering alone;
Ephraim has hired lovers (Hos 8:9–10).

Isaiah was in favor of complete neutrality, believing that trust in Yahweh's ability and willingness to save Judah would be betrayed by an alliance with Syria (Rezin), and Syria's junior partner, Ephraim (Pekah). This was Isaiah's oracle to Ahaz:

Take heed, be quiet, do not fear, and do not let your heart be
    faint (7:4).

Isaiah told Ahaz to trust completely in Yahweh. He informed Ahaz
that Rezin and Pekah were "smoldering stumps of firebrands," which
would soon burn out. Ahaz had to have faith in Yahweh. He warned
Ahaz that if he did not have faith in Yahweh he could not hope to have
his house established:

If you will not believe, surely you shall not be established
    (7:9).

In this sentence there is a play on two Hebrew words. It could be
translated like this: "If your faith is not sure (ta'aminu), your house
will not be secure (te'amenu)." The root of these two Hebrew words is
mn, which supplies us with the English word amen, which is a response meaning "I believe." We will discuss faith as a concept of
Isaiah in chapter 6.

STUDY QUESTIONS

1. If the vision of Isaiah was not an inaugural call, what other purpose
    could it have served?

2. What elements of temple worship were part of the vision?

3. What is the possible identity of "these people," and how would
    this interpretation soften the impact of the negative message from
    Yahweh to Isaiah?

4. Explain the purpose of the Syrian-Israelite coalition. What did the
    partners plan to do with Ahaz? Give some details.

5. Why did the house of David feel threatened at this time?

6. What was Isaiah's position on military alliances? What other
    prophet put forth a similar position? Give some scriptural support.

7. What evidence is there for the belief that the Memoirs of Isaiah
    may have been inserted in the center of a scroll containing a col-
    lection of oracles of Isaiah?

NOTES

1. John Hayes and Stuart Irvine make this point in their book *Isaiah, the Eighth Century Prophet* (cited above), pp. 108–109. They do this in support of their chronological interpretation of the entire book of First Isaiah, assigning all the social oracles (chapters 1–5) to the early period of Isaiah's activity. There is a social oracle contained in 10:1–4, however. It should have appeared as part of chapter 5.

2. The fact that the title is "Holy One of Israel," and not "Holy One of Judah," may indicate that the origin of the title dates from the days of David, or even earlier, when both kingdoms were called Israel.

3. For example see Robert Coote's *Amos Among the Prophets* (Philadelphia: Fortress Press, 1981), p. 62.

4. See p. 112 of the previously cited book on *Isaiah* by John Hayes and Stuart Irvine.

5. There is no agreement concerning the year of Uzziah's death. Depending on what chronology you consult, Uzziah died somewhere between 742 and 739 B.C.E.

6. Notice that the verse uses the words ". . . up to Judah." Judah was south of Israel and Syria, so we might expect the words to be "down to Judah." In the scriptures, however, there is a Jerusalem bias. When you went to Jerusalem, you always went "up to Jerusalem," because Jerusalem was identified with the mountain of God. In this verse, although the author says Judah, he had Jerusalem in mind.

7. The name of Isaiah's son, *Shear-jashub*, can be translated several ways, including "A remnant will return" and "Only a remnant will return." Some scholars interpret the first translation as good news and the second as bad news.

Chapter 6

THE MEMOIRS OF ISAIAH (CONTINUED)

Suggested Scripture Reading:

Isaiah 7:1–8:18

Take heed, be quiet, do not fear, and do not let your heart be faint (Is 7:4).

Following the vision of Isaiah, the first incident reported to us is the meeting between Isaiah, accompanied by his son Shear-jashub, and King Ahaz. The meeting place is identified as the end of the conduit of the upper pool. Ahaz may have gone there to inspect part of the city's water supply in the event of invasion by Syria and Israel.

The strange name of the son of Isaiah, Shear-jashub, is not explained or commented on to Ahaz in the narrative of the meeting between Ahaz and Isaiah. Perhaps it is to be assumed by the reader that Isaiah would introduce his son to Ahaz, and Ahaz would understand the symbolic meaning of the name. Later in the memoirs Isaiah would say, "See, I and the children whom the LORD has given me are signs and portents to Israel from the LORD of Hosts" (8:18). We remember that it is reported that Hosea had children with symbolic names also.

The name *Shear-jashub* is a one word sentence. It is often translated, "A remnant shall return." Because the subject comes first (not the usual order in Hebrew), the emphasis could be on the term "remnant," meaning, "*Only* a remnant shall return." But this meaning is not appropriate to the crisis of imminent invasion by Israel and Syria. Since no explanation of the name is given, and the name is not commented on here, it is possible that the name of the child would have

50

meaning for Ahaz at a future time, and not necessarily in conjunction with this present crisis. This is supported by the fact that the returning of a remnant as a subject appears later, following the memoirs, as a powerful prose oracle (10:20–27), and the theme of the remnant runs throughout Isaiah.

Some scholars have seen in the advice that Isaiah gave to Ahaz the birth of "faith" in the theology of the Old Testament.[1] In the account we are reading, Isaiah brings good news to Ahaz and encourages him to hold fast to his resolve not to join the anti-Assyrian coalition. It is not necessary to give in to the coalition. Its leaders will soon burn out. The coalition's threat to capture Jerusalem and replace Ahaz

> . . . will not stand,
>   and it will not come to pass (7:6).

Ahaz should trust in Yahweh. Evidently there was tremendous pressure from within Judah, on the house of David, to join the alliance. Isaiah was against it. The house of David will stand if Ahaz will trust Yahweh. Yahweh will preserve the house of David as he has promised. Isaiah believed that giving in to the alliance with Syria and Israel for protection against Assyria was evidence of lack of trust in Yahweh. The opposite to lack of trust was to have faith in Yahweh.[2]

Ahaz in the Deuteronomistic History

In 2 Kings 16 we are given facts concerning Ahaz which have to be dealt with. We can either synchronize the information in the Bible history with the accounts from Isaiah, or we can deny their validity.[3] Unfortunately there is no mention of Isaiah and his interaction with Ahaz in the historian's account of Ahaz's reign. (We will meet Isaiah in the Bible history during the reign of Hezekiah, 2 Kgs 18–20.) The history presents Ahaz as an evil king who sacrificed one of his sons. He also is reported to have "sacrificed and burned incense on the high places, and on the hills, and under every green tree" (2 Kgs 16:4). This is recognized as stereotypical language used by the Deuteronomistic historian for kings who were not good, in contrast with King Hezekiah, and particularly with King Josiah who was the *perfect servant of Yahweh*. Josiah destroyed the high places and the multiple shrines in his effort to centralize and standardize the worship of Yahweh (2 Kgs 23).

Here is the chief historical problem. We are told that Ahaz sent messengers to Tiglath-pileser saying:

> I am your servant and your son. Come up and rescue me from the hand of the king of Syria and from the hand of the king of Israel, who are attacking me. Ahaz also took the silver and gold that was found in the house of the LORD . . . and sent a present to the king of Assyria (2 Kgs 16:7–8).

Tiglath-pileser, it is inferred, accepted the offer of Ahaz to be his vassal, and marched against Damascus, defeating and killing Rezin. We are not told what happened to Pekah here, but elsewhere (2 Kgs 15:30) it is reported that Hoshea assassinated him and took the throne as a vassal of Assyria.

There are two problems. One relates to the historical reliability of Ahaz's appeal to Tiglath-pileser in 2 Kings 16, and the other to the memoirs of Isaiah, and Isaiah's theology.

(a) Judah was a very small country, considered by some an adjunct to Israel. It is highly unlikely that a king of Assyria would have come to rescue Judah as a response to a message from Ahaz. (b) There is no historical support for an appeal from Judah to Tiglath-pileser in the Assyrian inscriptions of that period.[4] (c) There is no specific condemnation in the writings of Isaiah directed to Ahaz concerning the message to Tiglath-pileser or concerning a Judean proposal for an alliance with Assyria which this move would have represented. How could Isaiah have condemned Ahaz for not trusting Yahweh if he allied with the anti-Assyrian coalition (Israel/Syria), and then have ignored the alliance with Assyria for protection against the coalition? It is impossible to believe that Isaiah would have winked at an alliance with Assyria at this time. But there is no hint of his condemnation.

The Sign of Immanuel

The immediate crisis was the threat to Ahaz and the house of David. We presume that Ahaz had doubts about accepting Isaiah's advice and found it difficult to believe Isaiah's good news concerning the sure downfall of the coalition, and that he continued fearful. So Ahaz was offered a sign from Yahweh. Ahaz replied that he would ". . . not ask, and I will not put the LORD to a test." Isaiah accuses the house of David of wearying God. It is not necessary to accuse Ahaz of false piety, as many commentators do, because of his refusal to request a sign. In and of itself, not asking for a sign from God may have been an act of positive virtue. When Isaiah responded with his statement about wearying God, he may have been referring to Ahaz's fearfulness and lack of trust. Regardless, Isaiah announces that the LORD will give a sign:

> Look, the young woman is with child and shall bear a son, and shall name him Immanuel . . . before the child knows how to refuse the evil and choose the good, the land before whose two kings you are in dread will be deserted (7:14–16).

At this point we encounter a much studied and much debated passage of scripture. There are many questions to be answered. Who is the young woman? Does the sign depend on the child's birth, the child's name, or the child's survival? Or all three? We may even ask a more basic question. Does the young woman's pregnancy have anything to do with the sign at all, or is it an additional oracle provided by the prophet?

About this last question there can be little doubt. If the pregnancy of the young woman and the birth of the child is not the expected sign, we would have every reason to expect that the sign to Ahaz would be identified later in the book of Isaiah, and this is not the case.

So a major question is: Who was the woman? Here are some answers: (1) The woman is Isaiah's wife, the prophetess. If this were true, then Isaiah had three children with symbolic names. Hosea is reported to have had three children with symbolic names.[5] (2) The woman is an anonymous woman, or even any young Judean woman who is pregnant at this time.[6] (3) The woman is seen in a vision of Isaiah, and as such cannot be identified. (4) The woman is a wife of Ahaz, and the child she bears will be an heir to the throne and will therefore continue the house of David.

Considering the importance here to Isaiah of the continuance of the house of David (and to Ahaz, to say the least), our logic leads us to side with those who identify the woman as a wife of Ahaz.[7]

In the northern kingdom of Israel, it was commonplace for a dynasty to be ended by a competing house.[8] And it was always an extremely violent, bloody act. For example, to end the house of Baasha:

> . . . he [Zimri] killed all the house of Baasha; he did not leave him a single male of his kindred or his friends (1 Kgs 16:11).

All male heirs had to be killed to put an end to the dynasty, and this included unborn children. And we know the coalition had plans to replace Ahaz with a foreign-born king:

> Let us go up against Judah and cut off Jerusalem and conquer it for ourselves and make the son of Tabeel king in it (7:6).

So the sign offered to Ahaz was about the survival of the house of David. His child, his heir, would survive, but his enemies, who plotted his removal, would not survive:

> For before the child knows how to refuse the evil and choose the good, the land before whose two kings you are in dread will be deserted (7:16).

A Reference to the Division of the Nation of Israel

Before the appearance in the text of four judgmental statements (7:18–25) there is an interesting reference to the time when Israel and Judah split from each other to form two independent kingdoms.

> The LORD will bring on you and on your people and on your ancestral house such days as have not come since the day that Ephraim departed from Judah—the king of Assyria (7:17).

What makes this verse interesting is that we have little detailed information in the Bible concerning the reaction of Judah to the departure of the ten northern tribes which had taken place after the death of Solomon. The split is reported in the Bible history in a matter-of-fact way as an almost bloodless coup. We are not told that these were particularly hard times for Judah; we are not informed of weeping, or wailing, or gnashing of teeth. But the verse in Isaiah seems to infer that they were terrible days. The key is in the phrase "your ancestral house." While the people of Judah may not have suffered hardship at the time of the split, the house of David certainly did. It was considered an unmixed tragedy in those times for a king to lose a large portion of his territory, as Rehoboam did, the heir of the house of David. Whether the lives of the people were improved or impoverished was not the issue from the king's point of view.

One commentator sees the possibility of good news in this verse.[9] He suggests that the original sentence referred to the days before the schism, when Israel and Judah were still united. In other words, the survival of the house of David raises the possibility of a reuniting of Israel and Judah under the reign of a Davidic king (Immanuel). There is a strong tradition that Hezekiah made attempts to reunite the territory of Israel with Judah (2 Chr 30:1–12).

But in this interesting verse we have a gloss, or *an explanatory note*, of which the book of Isaiah has many. An editor has given us his interpretation of the paragraph by adding the words, "the king of Assyria." One question we ask when we see a gloss such as this is, "When was it added?" It is easy to believe that it was added following the invasion of Judah by Sennacherib in 701. Since this editor has added the words "the king of Assyria" it is difficult for us to interpret the previous words in a positive way—unless, of course, the four judgmental statements which end the chapter, each beginning with the words *On that day*, refer only to Israel and Syria. It is true that no mention is made in them of Jerusalem or Judah, but only *the land* (v. 21). We will not be able to explain with finality many of the passages of Isaiah, but it is helpful to be familiar with their complexity and possible meanings.

Oracle Interpretation

Chapter 7 offers us an opportunity to become more self-conscious as students concerning our methods of oracle identification and interpretation. By this we mean that learning the natural divisions of a chapter will help us to interpret the text we are studying.

Chapter 7 is divided into four sections as follows:

(a) Narrative background of the crisis (1–6a).
(b) Isaiah's encouragement to Ahaz to stand firm (6a-9).
(c) The sign of Immanuel (10–17).
(d) A fourfold oracle of judgment (18–25).

We must always remember that the original Hebrew Bible was not written in chapters or verses. These divisions (chapters and verses) came hundreds of years later to assist scholars, in their studies, to communicate with each other. These divisions are quite functional and have survived for centuries because they serve a good purpose.

Because they are imposed on the text, however, they do affect the way the text is read and understood. It has become a habit for us to read to the end of a chapter and to stop there, for the day, or for a few minutes, as the case may be. For this reason our interpretation of an oracle is often influenced by another oracle which happens to be included in the chapter.

Chapter 7 closes with a fourfold oracle of judgment. Each section of this oracle begins with the words "On that day." What is going to happen "on that day" is devastating—for example:

> On that day every place where there used to be a thousand vines, worth a thousand shekels of silver, will become briers and thorns (v. 23).

Particularly vivid is the mention of a razor hired beyond the river (v. 20). Who did the hiring? Was it Ahaz or Yahweh? At any rate, this razor, identified as the king of Assyria, will shave off the hair of the head, the beard and the feet (private parts). This is a reference to the humiliating treatment of prisoners of war by a victorious army.

Because of the doom which these oracles predict, we are likely to go back and reinterpret parts of the previous oracles in the chapter. For example, it is said of the child Immanuel that he will eat curds and honey (v. 15). Is this the normal food of infants, or is it an indication of hard times for the people of Judah? In the closing section of the chapter, the people mentioned (who may not even be Judeans) will eat curds and honey because it is a time of calamity. Their farmland has been destroyed and they no longer have orchards, cornfields, the produce of their cultivated land, and the meat of their farm animals. With the closing oracle in mind, some commentators have interpreted the earlier verse concerning the child's diet as caused by the invasion of Assyria. But Assyria did not invade Judah in the reign of Ahaz. Would the reference to curds and honey eaten by Immanuel have been seen as indicating *hard times*[10] if the chapter had been divided differently, with this verse (v. 16) as the last?

> For before the child knows how to refuse the evil and choose the good, the land before whose two kings you are in dread will be deserted.

Here is the point. Books of eighth century prophecy are collections of poetic oracles. The order in which these oracles appear is not always clear to us. In modern times a collection of poetry could be arranged in many ways:

(a) Chronologically, with the earlier works first and later works following.
(b) By subject matter, with love poems in one section and patriotic or nationalistic poems in another.
(c) By length, with shorter works in one section.
(d) By type, with sonnets separated from odes, or narrative poems, and so forth.

The oracles of the Hebrew books of prophecy are also arranged in a deliberate order; unfortunately the reason for the arrangement is not always clear to modern readers. We are confused when we read a prophecy of hope, followed immediately by a prophecy of condemnation, or vice versa. And this happens frequently in the prophetic books. For example in Hosea we read oracles of punishment immediately followed by oracles of tenderness and love (Hos 2:13–14). When we look at the oracles in Isaiah, chapters 28–33, we will notice that they are arranged so that an oracle of judgment alternates with an oracle of hope.

Here are two suggestions. First, recognize that the oracles are part of a *collection*, and that any one oracle in Isaiah may not have a close, logical relationship to the oracle which precedes it, and, second, suspend or limit your demand for linear logic in reading prophecy. Prophecy is an art form, and art has a logic of its own which is not strictly related to the scientific method.

Summary

We are suggesting that the first three sections of chapter 7 can be interpreted in an entirely hopeful, optimistic way, even though the closing section of the chapter is judgmental. Some scholars are adamant in believing that the four part judgmental oracle using the introduction "On that day" cannot be attributed to Isaiah of Jerusalem.[11] We are saying that it is possible to attribute it to Isaiah. He may have delivered it at a different time, or it may apply to Israel, the northern kingdom, in which case it could certainly be an oracle of the period of the destruction of the Syro-Ephraimitic coalition.

The judgments imply the devastation of the land. As we continue into chapter 8 we will see clear references to Judah, but the land of Judah was not devastated by the Assyrians until the days of Hezekiah, particularly 701. Some scholars see the 701 invasion a result of decisions made by Ahaz at the time of the Syro-Ephraimitic crisis. We feel that it is reasonable to see a reading-back into the interaction of Isaiah and Ahaz, oracles which deal with the 701 invasion of Judah (thirty years later) by the Assyrians under Sennacherib.

STUDY QUESTIONS

1. What did Isaiah tell Ahaz when he met him at the end of the conduit of the upper pool?

2. Give three reasons which raise doubts concerning the historical accuracy of Ahaz' appeal to Tiglath-pileser for rescue.

3. Give four answers to the question, "Who was the woman, of whom Isaiah spoke, who would give birth to Immanuel?"

4. Why was the Bible divided into chapters and verses?

5. What is the significance of the sign of Immanuel, and why should it have calmed Ahaz?

6. What is the meaning of the name of Isaiah's child, Shear-jashub? What was the name of his other child? What other prophet is reported to have had children with symbolic names?

NOTES

1. We will speak about this in our chapter 12.

2. Otto Kaiser, for one, takes issue with the idea that Isaiah is a prophet of faith and trust. In discussing the narrative of chapter 7 he says it does not come from the prophet Isaiah, but belongs to the late sixth or early fifth century (*Isaiah 1–12*, p. 143).

3. John Hayes and Stuart Irvine in their commentary on *Isaiah, the Eighth Century Prophet* state that Ahaz could not have expected protection from Tiglath-pileser against the Syro-Ephraimitic coalition. They further argue that Ahaz was maligned by the Deuteronomistic historian, and that a ". . . more favorably disposed editor might have presented Ahaz in a favorable light" (pp. 42–46).

4. For a thorough discussion of this subject, along with an analysis of the message Ahaz is reported to have sent to Tiglath-pileser,

consult the book by John Hayes and Stuart Irvine, *Isaiah, the Eighth Century Prophet*, pp. 42–46. Also consult the dissertation by Stuart Irvine, *Isaiah, Ahaz, and the Syro-Ephraimitic Crisis*, Chapter Three, pp. 75–109.

5. For example, see the article by Peter Ackroyd, "The Book of Isaiah," in the *Interpreter's One Volume Commentary on the Bible*, p. 337. Also, see *Isaiah 1–39*, by R.E. Clements, p. 88. (However, many scholars interpret the word *almah* as a very young woman, and the implication is that this is her first child. Isaiah's wife already had a child, Shear-jashub. Isaiah could have married a second wife, of course.)

6. A serious student may want to consult a dissertation by Stuart A. Irvine, *Isaiah, Ahaz, and the Syro-Ephraimitic Crisis* (Atlanta: Scholars Press, 1990), pp. 168–169. Irvine has extensive footnotes on this and related subjects.

7. See the article co-authored by Joseph Jensen, O.S.B., in *The New Jerome Biblical Commentary* (Englewood Cliffs: Prentice-Hall, 1990), p. 235. Also see Hayes and Irvine, *Isaiah*, p. 136: "She is a Davidic princess, and her son to be born is a potential royal heir."

8. The house of Jeroboam lasted for two kings. The house of Baasha lasted for two kings also. The house of Omri (who established Samaria as the capital city of Israel) was ended by Jehu after four kings had reigned, one of whom was Ahab. The house of Jehu was the last significant dynasty in Israel. Four of the last six kings of Israel were murdered. See our chart entitled "Last Six Kings of Israel, The Northern Kingdom."

9. R.E. Clements, *Isaiah 1–39*, p. 89.

10. The article on Isaiah in the *New Jerome Biblical Commentary* comments on the mention of curds and honey in verse 15 as ". . . the only food available in a devastated land." This interpretation is influenced by the mention of curds and honey in 7:21 in a judgmental context. We can't always let scripture interpret scripture. There are several places in Isaiah where the same words have opposite connotations.

11. R.E. Clements, *Isaiah 1–39*, p. 89.

Chapter 7

THE END OF ISAIAH'S EARLY PROPHETIC ACTIVITY

Suggested Scripture Reading:

Isaiah 8

The memoirs of Isaiah start in 6:1 with the vision of Isaiah in the temple and end in 8:18 with the words

> I and the children whom the LORD has given me are signs and portents in Israel from the LORD of hosts, who dwells on Mount Zion.

The memoirs are not entirely in the first person. Notice that the memoirs open in the first person:

> In the year that King Uzziah died, I saw the LORD sitting on a throne, high and lofty . . . (6:1),

and end in the first person:

> See, I and the children whom the LORD has given me are signs and portents in Israel . . . (8:18).

Chapter 7 in its entirety is in the third person. Nevertheless we will accept the cohesiveness of the material and recognize the material as a unit.

With our identification of the memoirs as extending from 6:1 to

8:18,[1] we can construct a working outline of the first twelve chapters of Isaiah.

The Prologue to the Book	Chapter 1
A Collection of Early Oracles	Chapters 2–4
The Song of the Vineyard	Chapter 5:1–7
The First Six of Seven Woes	Chapter 5:11–23
The Memoirs of Isaiah	Chapter 6:1–8:18
The Ideal Davidic King	Chapter 9:2–7
A Liturgy of Discipline	Chapter 9:8–10:4
Oracles about Assyria	Chapter 10:5–10:34
A Shoot from the Stump of Jesse	Chapter 11
A Song of Praise	Chapter 12

Uriah the Priest: An Intriguing Peek into Cultic Practice

In the midst of the memoirs we have a reference to Uriah the priest which innocently reveals a speck of intriguing information for students of the Hebrew Bible.

> Then the LORD said to me [Isaiah], Take a large tablet and write on it in common characters, "Belonging to Maher-shalal-hash-baz," and have it attested for me by reliable witnesses, the priest Uriah and Zechariah son of Jeberichiah (8:1–2).

It may come as a surprise, but this passage opens a door, supplying the student with one of very few facts which we have concerning the ongoing practices of the Jerusalem cult of Yahweh in the pre-exilic period. In spite of all the information we have in the books of Leviticus and Numbers concerning sacrifices, tabernacle architecture, tabernacle furnishing, vestments, purification requirements, and required festivals, there are many reasons to doubt that the many requirements of these books of the Pentateuch were known, or widely practiced, in the temple of Jerusalem before the post-exilic period.[2]

Let us look at some of the information revealed to us by the reference to Uriah the priest and associated verses:

(1) Isaiah was instructed to make a large sign with a message on it to be posted for public reading. There is one other reference to this type of activity in the prophetic book of Habakkuk.

> The LORD answered me and said:
> Write the vision;
>> make it plain on tablets,
>> so that a runner may read it (2:2).

As to the purpose for these witnesses (Uriah and Zechariah) we can only speculate. Perhaps these were officials without whose approval a sign such as this could not be erected. Perhaps the date of the sign was what was being attested to. If the authenticity of the words were involved, it raises an interesting question about the possibility of an unauthorized prophet promoting a forgery. The fascinating element here is that this incident, along with a statement which follows (vv. 16–18), may be the earliest historical reference to recognition of writing as a revelation of Yahweh, the very beginning of the Hebrew Bible itself.[3]

(2) It is granted that we are dealing with some obscurity here. We cannot say for sure whether the tablet (which may have been clay[4] or a large piece of papyrus), contained only the words Maher-shalal-hash-baz, or whether this was the "heading," followed by additional words. The expression consists of two verbs meaning "hurry" and two nouns meaning "spoil." The RSV margin gives the translation, "The spoil speeds, the prey hastens." It foretells of a military defeat and has been compared with a popular military expression found in Egyptian writings, "Let the spoil hasten." We read earlier (5:26–30) a frightening description of the perfect invading army:

> None of them is weary, none stumbles,
>> none slumbers or sleeps,
> not a loincloth is loose,
>> not a sandal-thong broken (5:27).

Later, in chapter 10, when Assyria is described as a rod of punishment in the LORD's hand, we read:

Against a godless nation I send him,
    and against the people of my wrath I command him,
    to take spoil and seize plunder,
    and to tread them down like the mire of the streets (10:6).

The time of the invasion and the names of the defeated parties
are immediately identified in the present context:

Then the LORD said to me, Name him Maher-shalal-hash-
baz; for before the child knows how to call "my father" or
"my mother,"[5] the wealth of Damascus and the spoil of Samaria will be carried away by the King of Assyria (8:3–4).

(3) This event may mark the end of a period of prophetic activity
for Isaiah, after which he would withdraw for a while. He writes, "I
will wait for the LORD, who is hiding his face from the house of
Jacob, and I will hope in him."

The mention of "the house of Jacob" supports our contention
that in spite of the title found in 2:1, "The word that Isaiah son of
Amoz saw concerning Judah and Jerusalem," many of the early oracles had to do with, and referred to, the northern kingdom of Israel.
Even in explaining the song of the vineyard we read:

For the vineyard of the LORD of hosts is the house of
Israel . . . (5:7).

And further, in explaining what will be done to the vineyard, the
words apply to Israel in the eighth century and not to Judah:

And now I will tell you what I will do to my vineyard.
    I will remove its hedge, and it shall be devoured;
    I will break down its wall, and it shall be trampled down (5:5).

It is reasonable to believe that Isaiah spoke to the house of Israel with
prophetic words, just as Amos and Hosea had done. Sometime after
the destruction of Israel (722), the oracles were placed in their present order and the title of 2:1 mentioning "Judah and Jerusalem" was
added. The editor or editors of these oracles saw the infinite, and now
primary, value of these oracles for Judah and for Jerusalem. As to
when the prologue was added, and the psalm of praise which now
constitutes chapter 12 we cannot say. The beginning and end of this
early collection could have been added during the exile. If an exilic

edition of Isaiah contained the material of twelve chapters, then this scroll would have been about the same length as the final scrolls of Amos, Hosea, and Micah.

Much earlier than the exile of course, during the Syro-Ephraimitic crisis, a core of Isaiah's early oracles had been preserved:

> Bind up the testimony, seal the teaching among my disciples (8:16).

Did Isaiah Have a Circle of Disciples?

In conjunction with the sealing of Isaiah's teachings and the erection of the poster bearing the name of his son, there is a mention of "my disciples," which has stirred the imagination of Bible students for centuries. Did Isaiah have a circle of disciples, or a school of prophets like Elisha? Most scholars think not, and do not agree with the translation of the word as "disciples." Two reasons given are: (a) there are other ways to translate the Hebrew word translated disciples,[6] and (b) there is no further mention of a following for Isaiah, or a band of supporters, in the book of Isaiah or elsewhere in the Bible.

At this point Isaiah seems to be saying, "I will not be speaking further on the subject of the threat to Israel by Assyria, or the threat to Jerusalem by the coalition, but my name and the name of my two children will remind you of my teachings."

> See, I and the children whom the LORD has given me are signs and portents in Israel from the LORD of hosts, who dwells on Mount Zion (8:18).

The memoirs started with a vision of Yahweh in the temple, and end with reference to the LORD of hosts who dwells on Mount Zion.

The frightful, advancing army, previously referred to (5:26–30), had to be the Assyrian army coming to destroy Jerusalem's enemies, the coalition, including Syria and, unfortunately, Israel. But the throne of David would be preserved.

The End of the Coalition

In 734, Tiglath-pileser finished fighting off a threat from the Urartu, in his home territory of Mesopotamia, and headed for Palestine to deal with the coalition. The Assyrians were able to quickly

LAST SIX KINGS OF ISRAEL, THE NORTHERN KINGDOM

Name	Dates	Information
Zechariah	746–745	Murdered, after six month reign, by Shallum.
Shallum	745	Murdered, after one month, by Menahem.
Menahem	745–738	Accepted Assyrian rule and paid large tribute to Tiglath-pileser III.
Pekahiah	738–737	Assassinated by Pekah after two years.
Pekah	737–732	With Syria, tried to force Judah into an anti-Assyrian coalition. Tiglath-pileser reduced Israel to Samaria and the surrounding area (called Ephraim by Hosea and Isaiah).
Hoshea	732–722	At first paid tribute to Assyria, but later looked to Egypt for help in overthrowing Assyrian domination. Sargon II destroyed Samaria and made Ephraim an Assyrian province.

move down the coast, subduing Philistia and the area of Gaza. By doing this they were able to block any assistance to the coalition which may have been offered by Egypt or Ethiopia. In Hosea, Israel is accused of looking to Egypt for help.

> Ephraim has become like a dove,
>   silly and without sense;
>   they call upon Egypt. . . .
> Woe to them for they have strayed from me!

> Destruction to them, for they have rebelled against me (Hos 7:11–13).

It is quite possible that an assassination attempt against Ahaz was attempted in Jerusalem at this time. In 2 Chronicles we read:

> And Zichri, a mighty warrior of Ephraim, killed the king's (Ahaz') son Maaseiah, Azrikam the commander of the palace, and Elkanah the next in authority to the king (2 Chr 28:7).

The coalition had to withdraw from Jerusalem and give up its plan of replacing Ahaz. Tiglath-pileser was able to smash the coalition.

> The king of Assyria marched up against Damascus, and took it, carrying its people captive to Kir; then he killed Rezin (2 Kgs 16:9).

Hoshea killed Pekah (2 Kgs 15:30) and was able to take the throne of Ephraim as a vassal of Assyria.

Summary

In 734, as the Assyrians marched into the Palestine-Syria area under the leadership of Tiglath-pileser, Isaiah's first period of prophetic activity came to a close. Some important historical events reported to us from this period were not commented on by Isaiah. Facts concerning this period and the decade which followed have been outlined in our chapter 3. We will continue to comment on developing historical information in the next several chapters.

He watched as the parties in the coalition were humbled and destroyed by the army from the east. In his early years Isaiah was a prophet like Amos and Hosea. But his Jerusalem orientation and his background in Zion theology caused him to view certain things from a unique vantage point. He alone among the eighth century prophets was concerned with the survival of the house of David. When he resumed his prophetic activity he was almost entirely involved in the international political situation. As such, he may have been the first historical person in Israel to perceive of Yahweh not only as the God of Israel/Judah but as the God of all nations.

STUDY QUESTIONS

1. What was Isaiah instructed to write on a tablet? What did it mean?

2. Where was the tablet placed and what could have been the role of the two persons named in chapter 8?

3. Why do we believe that some of the early oracles of Isaiah refer to the northern kingdom of Israel?

4. What plans did the anti-Assyrian coalition have for Ahaz? Why?

5. What was the fate of the anti-Assyrian coalition?

6. Do you think Isaiah had a band of disciples? Why?

NOTES

1. See *The New Jerome Biblical Commentary*, p. 234. However, some commentators extend the memoirs through 9:7.

2. For one striking example we can take the important annual observance known as yom kippur, the day of atonement. This required observance is described in detail in Leviticus 16. Not once in the Deuteronomistic history is it referred to. Also there is no reference to it in the book of Deuteronomy. Both the Deuteronomistic history and the book of Deuteronomy predate the canonical books of Leviticus and Numbers.

3. There are references to writing the words of the Lord in earlier times, such as the reference in Joshua 24:26, "Joshua wrote these words in the book of the law of God," but there is no record of anyone ever reading this book of the law until it is discovered in the temple, in the days of Josiah (640–609 B.C.E.). Passages like this are not historical, but are idealized projections into the past.

4. R.E. Clements, *Isaiah 1–39*, says the tablet was a piece of dried clay (p. 94), but others say it was a large piece of papyrus.

5. The mother of the child is identified as the wife of Isaiah, the prophetess (8:3), and this is an interesting choice of words. A common Hebrew word for prophet is *nabi*. In the book of Isaiah, Isaiah never refers to himself, or is referred to, as a *nabi*, until the legendary narrative found in chapters 36–39, which was added to the Isaiah scroll a century after the death of Isaiah. But he does refer to his wife

using the feminine form of the word *nabi*. The word *nabi* is a favorite word for prophet in the Deuteronomistic History where it occurs over one hundred times. Robert R. Wilson, in his book *Prophecy and Society in Ancient Israel*, discusses the origin and meaning of this title, which he calls Ephraimitic. See pp. 136–138.

6. See Hayes and Irvine, *Isaiah*, pp. 160–169. "Those I have instructed" is suggested as a better translation by R.E. Clements, *Isaiah 1–39*, p. 100.

Chapter 8

THE ENTHRONEMENT OF
A PRINCE OF PEACE

Suggested Scripture Reading:

Isaiah 9–10

Ahaz maintained his neutrality and refused to join the anti-Assyrian coalition,[1] in spite of great pressure and threats from Israel and Syria, including an attempt to assassinate him (2 Chr 28:7), thereby putting an end to the house of David. Isaiah supported Ahaz in his neutral stand with oracles of assurance that the house of David would survive.

As the Assyrians arrived in the west to begin the ruthless and successful subjection of the entire area (734), Isaiah withdrew from public activity and watched as historical events unfolded. He would return as a powerful, new type of prophet sometime after the defeat of Damascus and Samaria.

Historical Information

We know that Ahaz paid tribute to Tiglath-pileser during this period.

Ahaz . . . took the silver and gold found in the house of the LORD and in the treasures of the king's house, and sent a present to the king of Assyria (2 Kgs 16:8).

An Assyrian tribute list from the period lists Ahaz of Judah among the

persons from whom Tiglath-pileser received tribute.[2] As expected,
there is no mention of tribute from the members of the coalition,
Syria, Israel, and Tyre.

Following the defeat of Rezin and Pekah (predicted by Isaiah
when he met the king at the end of the conduit of the upper pool,
7:3–8), Ahaz reported to Damascus to appear before Tiglath-pileser.
This visit to Assyrian-held Damascus lasted for some time, and was
probably for the purpose of "teaching" Ahaz how to be an Assyrian
vassal. An important incident took place at this time which we cannot
ignore:

> When King Ahaz went to Damascus to meet King Tiglath-
> pileser of Assyria, he saw the altar that was at Damascus.
> King Ahaz sent to the priest Uriah a model of the altar, and
> its pattern, exact in all its details. The priest Uriah built the
> altar; in accordance with all that King Ahaz had sent from
> Damascus, just so did the priest Uriah build it, before King
> Ahaz arrived from Damascus (2 Kgs 16:10–11).

When Ahaz arrived from Damascus, we are further told, he took the
bronze altar (mentioned in connection with Solomon's dedication of
the temple in 1 Kings 8:64), which was now between the new Syrian
altar (or Assyrian, we're not sure), and the house of the Lord, and
moved it to the north side of the newly erected Syrian altar (2 Kgs
16:14).

The whole matter of the altar is reported to the reader in a
matter-of-fact manner, and there is no criticism of the introduction of
a foreign altar into such a central place in the temple complex. Not
only was the Syrian altar built by the priest Uriah without objection,
but we have to note that there is not the slightest reference to this
significant cultic event in the subsequent oracles of Isaiah.

This incident is very important for our understanding of the days
of Isaiah, the eighth century. In our chapter 7 we commented on a
glimpse of temple practice involving the making of a poster by Isaiah
and stated that we know very little about the day-to-day happenings
in the temple of the eighth century. It is very easy for a beginning
Bible student to get the false impression that all the details relating to
the worship of Israel, especially as it relates to Jerusalem and the
temple, had been determined in previous, ancient times, and that
there was general agreement. All one had to do was to refer to ancient
writings to find out what was correct in God's eyes and what was not
correct. This impression is given because of the present content and

arrangement of the tetrateuch (the first four books of the Bible). In the closing chapters of the book of Exodus, and in Leviticus and Numbers, hundreds of cultic laws, rules, and regulations are found, covering every facet of worship imaginable, including offerings, priestly roles, purification ceremonies, temple architecture, furnishings, vestments, festivals, offerings, and so forth. What the student must keep in mind is that these books did not reach their final form until two to three hundred years after the eighth century. Many of the cultic rules which appear in Exodus, Leviticus, and Numbers, perhaps most of them, are idealized projections into Israel's legendary past.

This means that the eighth century was an extremely important, formative time for the religion and theology of Israel. Isaiah, Amos, Hosea, and Micah were the builders and makers of the faith. The records of their oracles are among the earliest historical documents we have for uncovering the developing religion of Judah. They were laying the foundation for a theological tradition which would develop into Judaism and Christianity. Although they were conservative, and looked to values in Israel's past, in no way were they simply interpreting an ancient body of laws and statutes. On the contrary, they were initiating the development of this great body of teachings which we know as the Hebrew Bible.

Examining Further the Structure of Isaiah 2 to 12

If the early oracles of Isaiah had been arranged chronologically, then the closing of the memoirs, specifically the passage where Isaiah declares that he and his children are signs and portents in Israel, may have completed the scroll. An editor decided on a different arrangement, however. A previous collection of oracles was taken, the approximate center was determined, and the memoirs were inserted.[3]

In doing this, the editor separated the last "woe" statement from the first six, and also separated a liturgical section, 5:24–25, from its place at the head of material continued in 9:8–10:4. We notice the repetitive refrain five times:

> For all this his anger has not turned away;
>   his hand is stretched out still (5:25; 9:12; 9:17; 9:21; 10:4).

We call the passage a liturgy because of the repeated refrain. It is easy to imagine a priest reading the five sections, and congregation members, or other priests, responding with the refrain. There is a similar five-part liturgy in the book of Amos where five former judgments are cited, each followed by a refrain, "Yet you did not return to me, says the LORD." In the Isaiah liturgy, each passage contains bad news for Israel, the northern kingdom.[4]

We should also note that a passage containing social/economic criticism ended up in chapter 10:

> . . . to turn aside the needy from justice and to rob the poor
> of my people of their right, that widows may be your spoil,
> and that you may make the orphans your prey (10:2).

We noted earlier that these passages, which resemble oracles found in the book of Amos, were found mostly in Isaiah, chapters 1 to 5.[5]

The arrangement of Isaiah 2–12 then is this. The memoirs supply the core. They are found at the center of the unit now identified as chapters 2 to 12. At one time, before the memoirs were placed in their central position (6:1 to 8:18), the oracles following the memoirs (continuing with 8:19) followed the material now located in chapter 5. The pre-memoirs arrangement had been determined because of the appearance of key words in the oracles. These key words are sometimes called catch-words.

The Catch-Word Principle

In an early scroll of Isaiah's oracles, before the insertion of the memoirs, these two oracles were next to each other:

(a) The approaching, invading army (5:26–30)
(b) The people consulting spirits (8:19–22)

These two oracles may not have originated with Isaiah at the same time, but were placed next to each other because they both contained references to (1) darkness, (2) distress, and (3) "looking to the earth":

> And if one look to the earth—
> Only *darkness and distress*;
> and the light grows *dark* with clouds (5:30).

> They will look to the earth, but will see only *distress and*

darkness, the gloom of anguish; and they will be thrust into thick *darkness* (8:22).

Furthermore, the great oracle concerning the prince of peace may have been placed in its present location, following the oracle about the people consulting spirits, because of the mention of darkness in its opening sentence.[6]

The people who walked in darkness have seen a great light (9:2).

The Prince of Peace

The people who walked in darkness have seen a great light;
    those who lived in the land of deep darkness—on them light
    has shined.
You have multiplied the nation,
    you have increased its joy;
they rejoice before you as with joy at the harvest,
    as people exult when dividing plunder.
For the yoke of their burden, the bar across their shoulders, the
    rod of their oppressor,
    you have broken as on the day of Midian.
For all the boots of the trampling warriors
    and all the garments rolled in blood
    shall be burned as fuel for the fire.
For a child has been born for us, a son given to us;
    authority rests upon his shoulders;
and he is named Wonderful Counselor, Mighty God,
    Everlasting Father, Prince of Peace.
His authority shall grow continually,
    and there shall be endless peace
    for the throne of David and his kingdom.
He will establish and uphold it with justice and with
    righteousness
    from this time onward and forevermore.
The zeal of the LORD of hosts will do this (9:2–7).

Many of the earlier oracles of Isaiah concerned the Israelites (northern kingdom). This oracle concerns the people of Judah, especially the house of David and Jerusalem. These are the ones on whom the light has shined (v. 2). Often in the Psalms, the blessing of Yahweh is compared with light.

The LORD is my light and my salvation (27:1).

Happy are the people . . . who walk, O LORD in the light of your countenance (89:16).

There are some scholars who think that "The people who walked in darkness" are the people of the far north, Zebulun and Naphtali, and the citizens of Galilee, who were the first to be separated from Israel by military enemies, first by the Syrians, then later by the Assyrians. The new king about to be enthroned would reunite the separated brothers and make it possible for them to enjoy once again the light of Yahweh's countenance. In 2 Chronicles 30:1–12 it is reported that Hezekiah held a great passover in Jerusalem to which he invited those of Israel who were left, even as far as Zebulun in the north. The response to his invitation was not great however.

Another explanation would interpret the people as the Judean supporters of Ahaz. After decades of subjection to Israel, and a period of real threat to the throne of David, the people of Jerusalem (the supporters of Ahaz) have had the bar across their shoulders and rod of their oppressor broken by Yahweh as in the day of Midian (v. 4). In the ancient days of the judges, the Midianites had oppressed the people of Yahweh for seven years until Gideon received a commission from Yahweh to "strike down the Midianites, every one of them" (Jgs 6:14–16). The boots and the bloody garments of the threatening army are good for nothing but to be burned in the fire. The poet in this hymn refers to the sound of the enemy army as the "tramping warriors." This would be fitting for a description of the advancing Israelites and Syrians. In his previous poem about the Assyrian army (5:26–30) he had referred to the horses' hooves and the wheels of the chariots as inspiring fear (5:28).

A Coronation Hymn

Because of the popular interpretation of this oracle as a messianic prophecy, it is easy for a reader to see verse 6 as a birth announcement or a prediction of a royal birth. The tense is past, however, and many scholars, following the lead of the German scholar Albrecht Alt, do not interpret this oracle as a birth announcement but as a coronation or enthronement hymn. It was believed that at the time of enthronement the king was adopted as a son of Yahweh:

> I have set my king on Zion,
>   my holy hill.
> I will tell of the decree of the LORD:
>   He said to me, "You are my son;
>   today have I begotten thee . . ." (Ps 2:6–7).

Also relevant to this interpretation are the words of Yahweh delivered to David by Nathan the prophet:

> He shall build a house for my name, and I will establish the throne of his kingdom forever. I will be a father to him, and he shall be a son to me (2 Sam 7:13–14).

Four enthronement names are given to the king:

> Wonderful Counselor
> Mighty God
> Everlasting Father
> Prince of Peace

These majestic titles, and many other titles of similar majesty, were commonly applied to the monarchs of ancient times. Well known is the fact that the Egyptian Pharaoh received five similar throne names at the time of his coronation.[7] Two throne names given to Egyptian kings were "Lord of Infinity" and "Prince of Eternity."

The purpose of the granting of throne names was to give the king a good start and to encourage the heart of the people and boost their confidence in the new king. These titles praised his wisdom (Wonderful Counselor), ascribed divinity (Mighty God),[8] promised his protection (Everlasting Father), and heralded days of peace and prosperity (Prince of Peace). The Hebrew word *shalom* implies peace and prosperity in all phases of life.

Not everyone identifies Hezekiah as the Davidic king for which this enthronement hymn was written. It is the most logical choice, however.[9] Hezekiah became sole king in 715 after a period of coregency which some scholars think reaches back to the days before the final destruction of Samaria (722).[10]

The enthronement hymn ends with a promise that the authority of this king would grow continually:

And there shall be endless peace for the throne of David and
his kingdom. . . . The zeal of the LORD of hosts will do this
(9:7).

His Hand Is Stretched Out Still

Following the enthronement hymn, the liturgy of the out-
stretched hand, which started in chapter 5, continues. The refrain is
repeated five times in all. An editor has added the following words to
make sure that the reader of the scroll understands its addressee, the
northern kingdom.

The LORD sent a word against Jacob, and it fell on Israel;
   and all the people knew it—
   Ephraim and the inhabitants of Samaria (9:8–9).

And later—

Manasseh devoured Ephraim, and Ephraim Manasseh
   and together they were against Judah (9:21).

Although the original oracles were against Israel, by the time they
reached the form in which we now have them, their purpose had
become a warning for Judah and Jerusalem.

All five sections contain descriptions of iniquity and of the judgments which were sent as punishment. The refrain is a harsh metaphor picturing a father beating a disobedient son. He has a rod in his
hand with which he strikes the one being punished. This was a practice of the times.

Those who spare the rod hate their children
   but those who love them are diligent to discipline them (Prov
   13:24).

Because Israel will not learn, "his hand is stretched out still."

This picture made a deep impression on the one who put together the prologue to the book, chapter 1. The prologue began with
a picture of rebellious children who despised the Holy One of Israel.
They would not learn from their punishment.

Why do you seek further beatings?

> Why do you continue to rebel?
> The whole head is sick,
>   and the whole heart faint (1:5).

There is no question concerning the identification of the rod. It is Assyria. In the next chapter we will examine, among other subjects, the boastful pride of the Assyrian invaders.

STUDY QUESTIONS

1. Read 2 Chronicles 28:7. Who tried to assassinate King Ahaz and why? Give your opinion.

2. What was the fate of Rezin of Damascus and Pekah of Samaria?

3. Why did Ahaz go to Damascus? What did Isaiah say about the foreign altar which Ahaz copied and commanded to be built in the Jerusalem temple complex?

4. The eighth century was a formative time in the development and growth of religion in Israel. Explain.

5. A book of eighth century prophecy is a collection of oracles. Why is it important for the reader to keep this in mind?

6. What are the memoirs of Isaiah? Where are they found and what do they contain?

7. A coronation hymn or enthronement hymn is found in Isaiah 9:2–7. What scriptures support this interpretation?

8. What are the four throne names given to the new king? What was the purpose of giving throne names at the time of coronation?

9. What evidence is there for the statement that a previous arrangement of oracles was opened for the insertion of the memoirs?

NOTES

1. See Hayes/Irvine, *Isaiah*, pp. 182–183 among others. In the dissertation by Irvine, *Isaiah, Ahaz, and the Syro-Ephraimitic Crisis* (Atlanta: Scholars Press, 1990), p. 109. "While many Judeans advocated cooperation with Rezin, the prophet strongly supported the

neutralist policy of Ahaz." While it is without a doubt that Ahaz became a vassal of Assyria, the point being made is that Ahaz did not appeal to Assyria for rescue from Israel/Syria as indicated in the Deuteronomistic History (DH).

2. See *ANET*, Volume I (Princeton: Princeton University Press, 1973), p. 193.

3. In English translation, if we exclude the prelude, there are eighty-three verses before the memoirs, and eighty-one verses following the memoirs. This is not a scientific way of dividing the Hebrew text, but it serves to illustrate that the memoirs are found in the approximate center of the early scroll.

4. It is not quite as clean as I present it here. The second passage, before the second appearance of the refrain, turns out to be the seventh "woe" statement, the one that was separated from the first six. This doesn't seem to be what we would expect. Somewhere in the production of the scroll there was possible scribal confusion.

5. Actually, the original oracles of Amos did not contain words like *justice, spoil*, and *prey*, but contained specific, picturesque phrases like ". . . they sell the righteous for silver, and the needy for a pair of shoes" (Am 2:6). When we find abstract words like *justice* in Amos, we look for the hand of a Josianic redactor.

6. The first verse of chapter 9 is prose and refers to the most northern territories of Israel. These territories were first taken from Israel by the Syrians and later by the Assyrians, reducing the land of Israel, the northern kingdom. As political troubles for Israel increased, other neighboring states further reduced Israel until only the territory of Ephraim remained. In the days of Isaiah and Hosea, Israel was often referred to as Ephraim. This prose statement (9:1) was not part of the oracle of the Prince of Peace which begins in 9:2.

7. See Kaiser, *Isaiah 1–12*, p. 212.

8. In the ancient world kings were believed to share various degrees of divinity. In Psalm 45 the king is referred to twice as God (v. 6 and v. 7), but we know from the great body of evidence that we have in the Hebrew Bible that the king in Jerusalem was never confused with Yahweh, or said to contain his attributes. The Hebrew root for God in Psalm 45 is *El*, not *YHWH*. The NEB translates the phrase "mighty God," accordingly: . . . in battle God-like.

9. Hezekiah is identified as the king in *The New Jerome Biblical*

Commentary, p. 237 and by R.E. Clements in *Isaiah 1–39*, p. 108. Also, see John J. Collins in the *Collegeville Bible Commentary*, the volume *Isaiah*, p. 34. However some commentators question the Isaianic authorship of the passage (Peter R. Ackroyd in the *Interpreter's One Volume Bible Commentary*, p. 338). Otto Kaiser argues for a post-exilic origin for this hymn (*Isaiah 1–12*, p. 217) written by priests or temple personnel who were familiar with copies of enthronement hymns and may have preserved a royal liturgy of Judah from the days of Isaiah. He would place it in the days of Nehemiah.

10. Hayes and Hooker in their *New Chronology* begin the reign of Hezekiah in 727, after the Syro-Ephraimitic crisis, but before the final destruction of Samaria. Irvine, in his dissertation, identifies Ahaz as the subject of the oracle, stating that Isaiah supported Ahaz from the beginning in his neutrality (p. 231). The oracle may not have been an enthronement hymn, but a hymn to celebrate the break of Ahaz and Jerusalem from the decades-long subjection to Israel.

Chapter 9

A SHOOT FROM THE STUMP OF JESSE

Suggested Scripture Reading:

Isaiah 10:5–11:16

Assyria is identified as the rod in the hand of the one who is providing punishment. However, ". . . the arrogant boasting of the King of Assyria and his haughty pride" will not escape the wrath of Yahweh (10:12). Isaiah quotes the Assyrian as saying:

> By the strength of my hand I have done it
> and by my wisdom, for I have understanding;
> I have removed the boundaries of peoples
> and have plundered their treasures;
> like a bull I have brought down those who sat on thrones (10:12).

Isaiah sees human pride as an abomination to the Lord. Assyrian pride will not go unpunished.

> The Sovereign, the LORD of hosts,
> will send wasting sickness among his stout warriors,
> and under his glory a burning will be kindled,
> like the burning of fire. . . .
> The glory of his forest and his fruitful land
> the LORD will destroy, both soul and body,
> and it will be as when an invalid wastes away (10:16–19).

The Remnant Will Return

Following the announcement that the pride of the Assyrians will be punished, we find the earliest meaning in the book of Isaiah of a

80

remnant. We remember that Isaiah's first son had a name which meant "a remnant shall return" (7:3).[1] In the original oracles of Amos and Hosea the concept of the remnant does not appear. In the book of Micah, references to a remnant cannot be assigned to Micah of Moresheth with assurance. If the prose paragraph (Is 10:20–23) speaking of the remnant of Israel belongs to Isaiah, it is unique among the eighth century prophets.

> On that day the remnant of Israel and the survivors of the house of Jacob will no more lean on the one who struck them, but will lean on the LORD, the Holy One of Israel, in truth. A remnant will return, the remnant of Jacob, to the mighty God (10:20–21).

This remnant consisted of Israelites who survived the Assyrian invasion by fleeing south to Judah, subjecting themselves to the Davidic king and thereby returning to Yahweh, the Holy One of Israel (10:20–21).

The concept of remnant will appear again following the oracle of the peaceful kingdom. At that time the concept will have a meaning exceeding the explanation given here. We will explain its expanded meaning after our comment on the stump of Jesse.

The Peaceful Kingdom

A shoot shall come out from the stump of Jesse,
   and a branch shall grow out of his roots.
The spirit of the LORD shall rest on him,
   the spirit of wisdom and understanding,
the spirit of counsel and might,
   the spirit of knowledge and the fear of the LORD (11:1–2).

The interpretation of this oracle depends on the translation and understanding of the Hebrew word *geza*, which appears in the Revised Standard Version as "stump." Many scholars explain the passage as originating during the period of late captivity when there was great hope in the exilic community for a divine revival of the house of David, or perhaps later, during the period of rebuilding in Jerusalem, following the return from captivity. At any rate, since the Davidic monarchy of Jerusalem had been destroyed by the Babylonians, the word "stump" means that the family tree of David had been cut down. Only a stump remained. From this stump, Yahweh would cause new life to appear. The point we are making here is that if the word is translated *stump*, meaning what is left after a tree has been cut down, then the passage is dated a century or more after the ministry of Isaiah. It becomes a late exilic, or post-exilic passage. But the word *geza* may be translated differently.

Another possible translation of the word *geza* is stem or stock. In Isaiah 40:24 the word refers to a recently planted tree with only a stem. In 11:1 the word *geza* is parallel to the word root. If the word could be translated *stem* or *root* of Jesse, then the oracle would not have to be dated after the destruction of Judah, but could be dated around 733, after the destruction of the coalition. And the branch upon whom ". . . the spirit of the LORD will rest" could refer to either Ahaz or Hezekiah.[2] After the punishment meted out to Israel by Assyria, Isaiah may have hoped for a reunion between the reduced Israel and Judah under the leadership of the Davidic king. This is stated in the chapter:

The jealousy of Ephraim shall depart,
    the hostility of Judah shall be cut off;
Ephraim shall not be jealous of Judah,
    and Judah shall not be hostile towards Ephraim (11:12–13).

Animals as Poetic Symbols

The wolf shall live with the lamb,
    the leopard shall lie down with the kid,
the calf and the lion and the fatling together,
    and a little child shall lead them (11:6).

The poetic imagery of this passage is so picturesque that it is not surprising that it has been widely known and widely misunderstood. Taken literally, it becomes a prediction of peace in the animal kingdom which has stirred the imagination of mankind and stirred deep emotions of hope for a beautiful world without danger. To take it literally, however, is to take the passage out of context. Isaiah was a prophet primarily concerned with the relationships between elements of human society. He used poetic symbols to express his hope for peace in his world. Bold poetic imagery appears frequently in the book of Isaiah; read the passage concerning the resurrection of the dead in Isaiah 26. It was the essence of Isaiah's poetic skills nurtured by his deep feelings and beliefs concerning the ultimate purposes of Yahweh, and the role which the house of David would play in these purposes, which gave birth to this poetry. The wolf, the leopard, the bear are strong animals who are predators in their natural state. When they are hungry they kill for food. Often young animals without protection are their prey, a lamb, a calf.

Amos used a figure of a lamb ripped apart by a lion to picture an enemy attack on Samaria:

> As the shepherd rescues from the mouth of the lion two legs,
> or a piece of an ear, so shall the people of Israel who live in
> Samaria be rescued, with the corner of a couch and part of a
> bed (Am 3:12).

A psalmist pictured an enemy army as a predator:

> When evildoers assail me *to devour my flesh*
> —my adversaries and foes—
> They shall stumble and fall (Ps 27:2).

Many centuries later Lord Byron continued the figure of invader as a wild animal:

> The Assyrian came down like a wolf on the fold.

Behind these poetic images lay a horrible reality.

The closing words reveal Isaiah's tribute to the ideal Davidic king as a prince of peace. The meaning of the pericope cannot be better stated than by using his own words:

> They will not hurt or destroy on all my holy mountain;
> for the earth will be full of the knowledge of the LORD as the
> waters cover the sea (Is 11:9).

The Spirit of the Lord

The prediction that ". . . the spirit of the LORD will rest on him" is very important. Earlier in the Bible history, in more ancient times, the spirit of Yahweh came upon individuals who played a role in fighting for the people of God, with Yahweh's blessing. In the Deu-

teronomistic History, the last person to have the spirit of Yahweh
come upon him was David:

> And the spirit of Yahweh came mightily upon David from
> that day forward (1 Sam 16:13).

With this in mind, the statement concerning this branch from the root
of Jesse takes on special significance.

The Remnant as a Religious Concept

The concept of the remnant is widely identified as one of the
unique characteristics of Isaiah's oracles, along with his use of the
phrase "Holy One of Israel." By contrasting the meaning and use of
the word remnant in the previous chapter (10:20–27), with its use in
this chapter (11:10–16), we can gain insight into the development of
a theological concept in the days of ancient Judah.

When Isaiah first used the word remnant he may have been referring primarily to "survivors" from the northern kingdom who fled to
the south, to Judah and Jerusalem, prior to and during the invasion of
Israel (722) by the Assyrians. The term remnant at that time was
primarily a political term. However, because those who fled came
chiefly to Jerusalem and its environs, their action came to be interpreted as a return to Yahweh. Since, in the eyes of Isaiah, Yahweh was
particularly and uniquely identified with the house of David and the
temple, there is some question concerning the legitimacy of the cultic
practices of these Israelites, coming from such northern cultic centers
as Shiloh and Shechem. Relocating in Jerusalem would be viewed as
returning to the Lord.

As soon as this was realized, the political term remnant began to
take on theological significance. It was only a short step to begin
understanding that out of the destruction of Israel some ultimate
good had been accomplished. Long separated brothers (this was a
male dominated society) were returning to Jerusalem and Yahweh.
And thus the early concept of a remnant, as part of the purpose and
plan of Yahweh was born.

Israel was destroyed in 722 and Judah survived. So far so good. A
century later, during the reign of Josiah, at a time when writing as a
revelation of Yahweh was about to come into its own, the Deuteronomic History appeared. Josiah, the perfect hero of Yahweh, from the
viewpoint of its author(s) and editor(s), appeared at the culmination

of its long story. At the same time there was a great interest in the oracles of the eighth century prophets. The scroll of Isaiah was studied and updated. The concept of remnant was one of its unique characteristics.

With the tragic and unexpected death of Josiah, the theology of the Deuteronomists, to whom Josiah represented the culmination of Yahweh's plan for his people, was in an immediate need of a revision and an updating. Only twenty-two years after the sudden and unexpected death of Josiah, the city of Jerusalem and the temple of Yahweh lay in ruins. The chief citizens of Jerusalem were carried away into humiliating captivity in 586.

As the years passed, the Isaian concept of a remnant was studied and reconsidered. It had to be applied to the defeated people of Judah, wherever they were. The word remnant took on weighted theological meaning. In the eighth century the word remnant did not refer to the people who used the word. It had been used by the Judean prophet Isaiah to speak of the survivors of Israel, the northern kingdom. Following the destruction of Jerusalem, the word remnant did not refer to a third party. The term, the concept, was used by the people of captivity who applied the word to their own status. Belief in a remnant was necessary to encourage hope and ensure faith in Yahweh's plan for his disciplined people.

Summary

In chapters 2 through 12 we found assorted oracles dealing with the following subjects:

(a) Condemnation of societal practices which produced economic hardship for the masses of Judah and Israel.
(b) Promises that the house of David would survive.
(c) Encouragement for the house of Ahaz to have faith in Yahweh.
(d) Attacks on human pride and arrogance.
(e) Oracles in the form of a public reading (liturgy) concerning judgments on Israel which she should have heeded but did not.
(f) Oracles of woe predicting the devastation of Israel, the northern kingdom, and the use of Assyria as the rod of Yahweh.

(g) Statements concerning a remnant which would return to
    Yahweh.

STUDY QUESTIONS

1. The early use of the word remnant referred to survivors of the
   northern kingdom. Locate a scripture passage which may illustrate this.

2. In Isaiah 11:1 there is a statement concerning "the stump (*geza*) of
   Jesse." Explain how the translation of the word *geza* affects the
   dating of the oracle.

3. Why is it significant that "the spirit of the Lord" will come upon
   the branch?

4. In your opinion, who is the branch?

5. How do you interpret the oracle beginning with the words "The
   wolf and the lamb shall live together"?

6. Explain how the word remnant may have changed its meaning as
   the status of Israel and Judah changed.

NOTES

1. In 7:3 the name of Isaiah's son is not translated. He is called
Shear-jashub. The translation, "a remnant shall return," is supplied in
the margin of the NRSV.

2. See Hayes and Irvine, *Isaiah, the Eighth Century Prophet*, pp.
212–213. The authors state that if the word is translated stump it
could refer to the reduced state of the Davidic territory during
Isaiah's early years (735/4). They identify the branch as Ahaz.

Chapter 10

ORACLES CONCERNING THE NATIONS

Suggested Scripture Reading:

Isaiah 13–23

The section of Isaiah consisting of chapters 13 through 23 is traditionally entitled "Oracles Against the Nations." This is not the best title for this section which contains a variety of material. When we think of oracles against a nation we are likely to think of a divine curse. Not every oracle is "against" the nation mentioned. A lament concerning the suffering of Moab appears in chapter 15 where the author seems to be sympathizing with the sufferings of the Moabites. A prose section is located in chapter 19 (vv. 18–24) which is entitled "Egypt, Assyria, and Israel Blessed" in a popular edition of the NRSV. If by nations we understand foreign nations, then we are surprised to find an oracle directed against Judah in chapter 22, followed by a prose section dealing with Jerusalem's internal politics. If we exclude chapter 22, however, and the opening paragraph of chapter 20 (where Isaiah is commanded to wear nothing more than what a prisoner of war would wear), we could accurately call the whole section "Prophesies Which Mention Foreign Nations."

The form of literature which the modern Bible student encounters when reading the eighth century prophets produces what can be called a rough ride over uneven terrain. We live in an age of comfort and smoothness, where temperature is controlled, noise is called pollution, and electronic speakers are everywhere, surrounding us with soothing music to calm our nerves. Reading a Hebrew prophet is usually not a soothing experience, however, and this is doubly true when we read prophetic oracles concerning the nations.

For one thing, in addition to our lack of interest in Moab, Tyre, and Edom, it seems that these oracles always appear in collections, one after another, so we encounter them in large doses. This is true in Jeremiah (chapters 46–51) and in Ezekiel (chapters 25–32), and, to a lesser extent, in Amos (chapters 1–2). Another thing that disturbs us is the vehemence of the curses which are pronounced on the population of these countries. Although we know little of Moab, we don't enjoy reading:

> Kir is laid waste in a night,
>   Moab is undone . . .
> On every head is baldness,
>   every beard is shorn;
> in the streets they bind on sackcloth;
>   on the housetops and in the squares everyone wails and melts
>   in tears (15:1–3).

For the people of Egypt we do not want to contemplate the following:

> The waters of the Nile will be dried up,
>   and the river will be parched and dry; its canals will become
>   foul,
>   and the branches of Egypt's Nile will diminish and dry up,
>   reeds and rushes will rot away. . . .
> Those who fish will mourn;
>   all who cast hooks in the Nile will lament,
>   and those who spread nets on the water will languish.
> The workers will be dismayed,
>   and all who work for wages will be grieved (19:5–10).

Even worse are violent passages such as this:

> Whoever is found will be thrust through,
>   and whoever is caught will fall by the sword.
> Their infants will be dashed to pieces before their eyes;
>   their houses will be plundered,
>   and their wives ravished (13:15–16).

The truth is that oracles against the nations are part of the Hebrew Bible and we have to put forth an effort to understand their role if we want to understand the culture of the near and middle east in ancient times. Edgar W. Conrad in a recent book on Isaiah, *Reading Isaiah*,[1] addresses this problem. Writing about the final verse of the book of Isaiah as typical of passages found in the oracles,

> And they shall go out and look at the dead bodies of the people who have rebelled against me; for their worm shall not die, their fire shall not be quenched, and they shall be abhorrence to all flesh (Is 66:24),

he writes,

> To contemporary readers who are horrified by the Jewish holocaust, the killing fields of Cambodia, and Tiananmen Square in China, some of the imagery of the book is horrifying. . . . I don't know what to do with this verse. I want to delete it as well as others of its kind. To do so, however, would be to engage in the process of remaking Isaiah in the refinishing school of Western good taste. It would be to eliminate its distance. Strategies for reading Isaiah must assert both the text's presence and its distance.

The fact that the oracles appear in collections may give us a clue to understanding their function. They probably served a liturgical function, and in some form were read publicly at annual festivals. People expected prophets to denounce foreign nations. In fact, during the last decades of Judah's political existence, Jeremiah referred to this prophetic activity:

> The prophets who preceded you and me from ancient times prophesied war, famine, and great pestilence against many countries and great kingdoms (Jer 28:8).

Judah was a small, weak nation, surrounded by nations large and small, which frequently attacked and plundered. Borders were pushed back, tribute was demanded, treaties were broken, resources were stolen, populations were brutalized. The fact that there are collections of oracles against the nations in Amos, Isaiah, Jeremiah, and Ezekiel prove that they served a function in the rituals of the culture.

Lawrence Boadt in a commentary on Ezekiel[2] explains three purposes served by oracles against the nations.

These oracles served several purposes. One was to underscore that Yahweh, the God of Israel, was also Lord of the nations and held other nations accountable for the deeds just as he did Israel. Another was to demolish foreign claims to divine authority by showing that they acted out of human pride, hubris, when they pitted their divinities (Marduk, Baal, or others) against Yahweh. Their pretensions would be demolished and brought to utter lowliness. A third purpose was to reassure the Israelites themselves that the attacks and oppression of these nations against God's chosen people would not go unpunished.

Benefits for the Student Who Reads These Oracles

There are good reasons for the modern student to read carefully the oracles against the nations in Isaiah.

(a) They will paint a picture for us of the history of the time, even if this is partial, one or two strokes at a time.

(b) As we read, if we are alert, we can catch glimpses of everyday life in ancient times. For example, as we read about the drying up of the Nile above, we were reminded of how dependent Egypt was on the Nile, and we were told of those who fish by casting hooks and those who spread nets. There are many of these glimpses. Of those who live in the Negeb desert we read:

They prepare the table,
    they spread the rugs,
    they eat, they drink (21:5).

We are given a picture of the merchant activity of the Sidonians:

O merchants of Sidon,
    your messengers crossed over the sea
    and were on the mighty waters;
your revenue was the grain of Shihor,
    the harvest of the Nile;
you were the merchants of the nations (23:2–3).

In the oracle concerning Ethiopia (chapter 18) we have an intriguing reference to "vessels of Papyrus on the waters," and a lovely description of the Ethiopians as "a people tall and smooth."

(c) The most important contribution which a reading of the oracles will make for us has to do with the picture of the ancient world from the viewpoint of a Judean. In making an outline of the nations referred to in chapters 13–23 a map of that ancient world emerges.

13:1–14:23	Babylon
14:24–27	Assyria
14:28–32	Philistia
15:1–16:4	Moab
17:1–14	Damascus (and Ephraim)
18:1–20:6	Egypt
21:1–10	Babylon
21:11–12	Edom
21:13–17	Arabia
23:1–18	Tyre

In Isaiah 11:12 we read:

He will raise a signal for the nations,
    and will assemble the outcasts of Israel,
and gather the dispersed of Judah
    from the four corners of the earth.

The expression *four corners of the earth* is still a common expression today in a modern, scientific age. Today, however, it is poetry; in ancient Judah it was geography.

It is helpful for the student to keep in mind that the world of the Hebrew prophets was a much smaller world than the one we live in today. For the ancient Judean this world did not extend further east than Persia, and westward to Egypt in northern Africa, the islands of the Mediterranean, and Anatolia (Turkey) to the northwest. Not only was the *geographic* world very small, but the entire universe consisted of only a small earth, with heaven above and Sheol below. This severely limited universe, and the mythology bound to it, is also revealed in the "oracles against the nations." Speaking of the king of Babylon we read:

You said in your heart,
"I will ascend to heaven;
    I will raise my throne
    above the stars of God;
I will sit on the mount of assembly
    on the heights of Zaphon;[3]
I will ascend to the tops of the clouds,

I will make myself like the most high."
But you are brought down to Sheol,
　　to the depths of the Pit (14:13–15).

Problems with These Oracles Against the Nations

We have stated above that oracles against the nations were functional and served a purpose in ancient Israel. We have also pointed out good reasons for the student to read these oracles. Now we must discuss some problems concerning them.

First, they are not of uniform length. A section identified in a popular edition of the NRSV as "An Oracle Concerning Philistia" is five verses long. Immediately following there is a section called "An Oracle Concerning Moab." It is twenty-two verses long. Second, the oracles do not share a common format. Without an identifiable format we often cannot identify a beginning and an end for the oracle. In other words, what we have is a series of collected prophecies from different times, by different authors, about these foreign nations.

Third, in chapter 22 there are no foreign nations identified. In the first half of the chapter Jerusalem is mentioned, and the second half of the chapter is a prose section dealing with internal politics of Jerusalem concerning two persons named Shebna and Eliakim. This last problem can be dealt with simply by speculating that chapter 22 is out of place. By switching chapter 22 with chapter 23, which is a collection of prophecies about Tyre, the complete collection of the prophecies concerning the nations would be contiguous.

The First Oracle

We will examine the first of the oracles against the nations. Chapter 13 begins with a title:

The oracle concerning Babylon that Isaiah son of Amoz saw (13:1).

Without this title the reader would not know until verse 19 that Babylon was a subject. The next chapter, 14, begins with a short prose statement about the restoration of the house of Jacob, and then continues with a taunt song against the king of Babylon. The first collection of prophesies against the nations seems to contain forty-one verses against Babylon. This would make it the largest collection of prophesies against a nation in First Isaiah. Why would Isaiah, an eighth century prophet, direct so many words against Babylon, a foreign power which would not come into its own as a political threat to the area and a threat to Judah for another century?

Many scholars have asked this question and have answered by explaining that the bulk of this collection of prophecies against Babylon must be dated much later than Isaiah, after the destruction of Jerusalem in 587. But there is another answer, depending on the identification of the king of Babylon. In 729, several years after the defeat of Rezin of Damascus, and after the trip of Ahaz of Judah to appear before Tiglath-pileser in Damascus (2 Kgs 16:10), Tiglath-pileser marched into the city-state of Babylon and made himself king of Babylon. Tiglath-pileser's name as king of Babylon was Pulu, or Pul. He is called Pul in a passage from 2 Kings:

> King Pul of Assyria came against the land; Menahem gave
> Pul a thousand talents of silver, so that he might help him
> confirm his hold on the royal power (2 Kgs 15:19).[4]

Tiglath-pileser died two years after declaring himself king of Babylon, in 727. This was the same year that King Ahaz of Judah died. This is significant, because in the same chapter where the taunt song against the king of Babylon ends, this verse appears:

> In the year that King Ahaz died this oracle came (Is 14:28).

What we are told in the above verse is that Isaiah was composing prophesies against the nations in 727. So it is not outside the realm of possibility that the king of Babylon in the taunt song of chapter 14 was indeed Tiglath-pileser, and that Isaiah was the author.

There is reason to believe that this oracle concerning Babylon may have been brief in its original form. Considering the role which Babylon played in the history of Judah a century after Isaiah's death, it is not difficult to imagine that scribal editors would add to this oracle. In its final form it is forty-four verses long, and seems to be composed of several smaller oracles. At the end someone has placed a prose summary:

> I will rise up against them, says the LORD of hosts, and will
> cut off from Babylon name and remnant, offspring and pos-
> terity, says the LORD. And I will make it a possession of the

hedgehog, and pools of water, and I will sweep it with the broom of destruction, says the LORD of hosts (Is 14:22).

Did Isaiah Write These Oracles?

We have stated that these oracles are accurately described as collections of prophecies which mention foreign nations. Many scholars attribute some of the material to Isaiah and other material to later authors and editors. For example, George Fohrer in his *Introduction to the Old Testament*[5] attributes to Isaiah prophecies concerning Assyria, Philistia, Damascus and Ephraim, and Egypt. He also attributes to Isaiah chapter 22 dealing with Shebna and Eliakim and the internal politics of Jerusalem. Like many other scholars he sees the opening collection of prophecies dealing with Babylon as late exilic.

Our position is that the core of these prophecies is made up of genuine Isaianic oracles. There is little doubt that editors have gathered and arranged the material, expanding it by adding editorial comments. Here is an example of an expanded passage. In chapter 22 a positive statement is made about Eliakim:

> I will fasten him like a peg in a secure place, and he will become a throne of honor to his ancestral house (22:23).

Evidently, subsequent events did not support this hope, so the passage ends with the editorial addition of this negative comment:

> On that day, says the LORD of hosts, the peg that was fastened in a secure place will give way; it will be cut down and fall, and the load that was on it will perish, for the LORD has spoken (22:25).

Summary

Although the collections of oracles appearing in chapters 13 through 23 (with the exception of chapter 22) are traditionally called "oracles against the nations" these chapters can be more accurately described as collections of prophecies which *mention* foreign nations. For example, chapter 15, for the most part, contains a lament for the suffering of Moab:

My heart cries out for Moab. . . .
   the waters of Nimrim are a desolation;
the grass is withered, the new growth fails,
   the verdure is no more (15:5–6).

Many of these prophesies were written by Isaiah and were later expanded and arranged by seventh century and sixth century scribes.

STUDY QUESTIONS

1. Where are the oracles against the nations found in the book of Isaiah? Name three other books which contain collections of similar oracles.

2. What does the fact that there are four collections of oracles against the nations tell us?

3. What are the benefits to reading oracles against the nations?

4. The first oracle in this collection mentions the king of Babylon (14:3). Could Isaiah have written this oracle? Explain.

5. Did Isaiah write these oracles? Explain your opinion.

6. Read the comments about Eliakim in 22:23 and 22:25. How do you account for the contradiction?

7. Explain the Judean view of the world and the universe.

NOTES

1. Edgar W. Conrad, *Reading Isaiah* (Minneapolis: Fortress Press, 1991), p. 162.

2. See "Ezekiel" in *The New Jerome Biblical Commentary* (Englewood Cliffs: Prentice-Hall, 1990), p. 321.

3. Mount Zaphon was in Syria, north of Israel. It was believed to be the earthly counterpart of a heavenly Mount Zaphon where Baal had his castle built with El's permission.

4. For a picturesque description of Menahem in words attributed to Tiglath-pileser, see *The Ancient Near East*, ANET (Princeton: Princeton University Press, 1958), p. 194.

5. Georg Fohrer, *Introduction to the Old Testament* (Nashville: Abingdon, 1968), pp. 367f.

Chapter 11

THE APOCALYPSE OF ISAIAH

Suggested Scripture Reading:

Isaiah 24–27

The four chapters following the Oracles Against the Nations are widely viewed by scholars as an integral unit. Chapters 24 through 27 form a unit traditionally called The Apocalypse of Isaiah.[1] Some characteristics of apocalyptic writing are found here, and for this reason many scholars have stated that these chapters constitute the latest section of the entire book of Isaiah, even later than the oracles assigned to the post-exilic author known as Third Isaiah (56–66).[2] John Collins, in an article entitled "Old Testament Apocalypticism and Eschatology" in *The New Jerome Biblical Commentary*, does not entertain the possibility that this unit (Isaiah 24–27) could have originated in the eighth century. He cites the possible date as being anywhere from two hundred years after Isaiah to four hundred years after Isaiah.[3] In our discussion, however, we will suggest that Isaiah was the author of at least the core of the unit.

Why This Unit Has Been Called an Apocalypse

The reasons given for using the word apocalypse for these chapters include the following: (a) In contrast with many of the oracles in the preceding section (chapters 13–23), which are addressed to particular nations, the powerful oracle opening this unit has as its subject the whole earth.

97

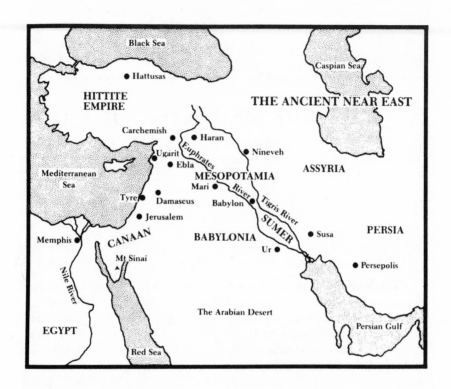

Now the LORD is about to lay waste the earth
    and make it desolate. . . .
The earth shall be utterly laid waste and utterly despoiled;
    for the LORD has spoken this word.
The earth dries up and withers,
    the world languishes and withers;
    the heavens languish together with the earth (24:1, 3–4).

In another passage the destruction of the earth appears as elements in a list. The list is a common literary form used throughout the
book of Isaiah.

The earth is utterly broken,

the earth is torn asunder,
the earth is violently shaken,
    the earth staggers like a drunkard (24:19–20).

(b) Yahweh will not only destroy the whole world, he will destroy the hosts of heaven (24:21), and will also destroy Leviathan, "the dragon that is in the sea" (27:1). Leviathan was a mythological sea monster which played a role in Mesopotamian and Canaanite (Ugaritic) folklore. In apocalyptic literature there is often reference to the defeat or slaying of a symbolic beast representing chaos or an evil power. The reference to the hosts of heaven is obscure, but by mentioning them the whole world is covered, not only from east to west, but also from above the earth to below the earth, Leviathan being understood as a creature of the deep oceans. This introduces a cosmic element common in apocalyptic literature. It is probable that an extended Canaanite mythology was prevalent in pre-exilic Israel, a mythology which has not survived in the present Hebrew canon.

(c) In apocalyptic literature, after a period of destruction and great suffering, there follows the dawn of a new age, or the creation of a new earth (Rev 21:1). This element is present in these four chapters also. On the mountain of the Lord there will be a feast, and God will wipe away the tears from all faces (see Rev 21:4). This is the beginning of the new age.

(d) Another element in apocalyptic literature is the resurrection of the dead:

Your dead shall live, their corpses shall rise.
    O dwellers in the dust, awake and sing for joy!
For your dew is a radiant dew,
    and the earth will give birth to those long dead (26:19).

In the book of Daniel, an apocalyptic book, we have this reference to a resurrection:

Many of those who sleep in the dust of the earth shall awake,
some to everlasting life, and some to shame and everlasting
contempt (Dan 12:2).

Can These Four Chapters Be Better Identified?

After having described this unit by the widely used title, *The Apocalypse of Isaiah*, and having given several reasons for using this title, we now have to explain why many scholars are not comfortable with the description of the unit as an apocalypse. An author of a popular article on Isaiah declared emphatically: "These chapters are not apocalyptic."[4]

There are several, interrelated reasons for not considering these chapters as apocalyptic literature:

(a) True apocalyptic literature, such as that found in Daniel 7 to 12, and in the book of Revelation, has a person who sees visions and reports these visions:

> I Daniel saw in my vision by night the four winds of heaven stirring up the great sea (Dan 7:2).

And John in Revelation states:

> After this I looked and there in heaven a door stood open! At once I was in the spirit (Rev 4:1).

In this unit the author does not report seeing visions.

(b) Apocalyptic writing, beginning in the post-exilic period, does not simply make use of symbolism, but is made up of elaborate symbolism tied into a structure of numerology. In Daniel there are four beasts, one beast with ten horns, a reference to 2,300 evenings and mornings, and another reference to seventy weeks. Significant numbers do not appear in the so-called Isaiah apocalypse.

(c) Although the Isaiah unit begins with an eschatological theme, the destruction of the earth, this theme, and others which appear in the four chapters, also appear in the first twenty-three chapters, and can be called typical prophetic themes.

It is true that the opening paragraphs speak of the punishment of the whole earth, but the previous chapters said the same thing, except that in the preceding chapters the desolation was described one nation at a time. When you put all the nations mentioned in chapters 13–23 together, you have the whole earth. We should remind ourselves that the "whole earth" from the viewpoint of ancient Judah was a very small place. It went as far east as Persia and as far west as the islands of the Great Sea. Heaven was above, and Sheol below, and that was the universe. There was one sun, a moon, and the actual size and nature of stars were not imagined.

An analysis of the oracles of the unit (24–27) discloses many typical prophetic themes, many of which already appear in the first twenty-three chapters of Isaiah. It is possible to read the unit as a

poetic summary of all the oracles which precede it in the book of
Isaiah. Yahweh punishes the earth because of the crimes of the people
of the earth and because of human pride. The mountain of the Lord is
then exalted:

> . . . the LORD of hosts will reign on Mount Zion and in Jeru-
> salem. . . . On this mountain the LORD of hosts will make for
> all peoples a feast of rich food (24:23; 25:6).

The scattered of Israel will return from Assyria and Egypt to the holy
mountain of Jerusalem (27:13). The nation of the Lord's people will
prosper without fear of invasion.

> But you have increased the nation, O LORD,
>   you have increased the nation;
> you are glorified;
>   you have enlarged the borders of the land (26:15).

The Date of This Unit

Although traditionally many scholars have recognized the four
chapters under discussion as a unit, this does not mean that there have
not been editorial additions and expansions. The specific mention of
Moab in 25:10b–12 seems to be out of place if the unit is indeed a
summary of all the preceding oracles.

Another description of the unit has been offered by Hayes and
Irvine in their commentary on *Isaiah, the Eighth Century Prophet.*
Their chapter on this unit is entitled "A Cantata of Salvation."[5] It is
quite possible that what we have in this unit is a liturgical composition, a collection of songs and chants, written by Isaiah for a time of
celebration in the temple during a period of peace and hope for Judah
and the city of Jerusalem. We look to the history of Assyria to determine when this period of celebration may have taken place.

In the Bible history we are told that the Assyrian king, Shalmaneser, came against Samaria and took Hoshea prisoner several years
before the destruction of Samaria (722).

> Assyria found treachery in Hoshea; for he had sent messen-
> gers to King So of Egypt, and offered no tribute to the king of
> Assyria (Shalmaneser), as he had done year by year; there-

fore the king of Assyria confined him and imprisoned him
(2 Kgs 17:3–4).

Shalmaneser died in 722. Although the name of his successor, Sargon
II, is not mentioned in the Bible history, there is no doubt that it was
Sargon, the new Assyrian king, who completed the destruction of
Samaria and was the person who arranged for the Israelites to be
carried into captivity.

For almost two decades Sargon was kept busy on several military
fronts including (a) the city-state of Babylon, (b) an area north of the
Mediterranean (Anatolia), and (c) the Egyptian Delta area. In spite of
opposition from several fronts, Sargon was able to control trade by
land and sea. Trade between Egypt and Assyria became brisk, and this
development may have provided the background for the oracles of
Isaiah concerning interaction between Egypt and Assyria:

> On that day there will be a highway from Egypt to Assyria,
> and the Assyrian will come into Egypt, and the Egyptian into
> Assyria (Is 19:23).

Control of commerce by Assyria could not have been beneficial to
Judah and the other small nations of the Palestine/Syria area. It is
quite possible that Assyrian efforts in the Mediterranean area were
supported by forced tribute from local nations including Judah.

In 705 Sargon was killed while leading an army of Assyrians to
deal with a problem in Anatolia. His death resulted in widespread
rebellion and optimism for the near east which included the small
nation of Judah. There was hope and expectation of Assyria's decline.
Reports of people celebrating throughout the area reached Isaiah
who saw the will of Yahweh being fulfilled:

> . . . they shout from the west over the majesty of the LORD.
> Therefore in the east give glory to the LORD;
>   in the coastlands of the sea glorify the name of the LORD, the
>   God of Israel.
> From the ends of the earth we hear songs of praise (Is 24:14–16).

It is believed that Hezekiah was a leader of rebellion against Assyria
in 705. Hezekiah had plans to extend the borders of Judah. Isaiah had
foreseen and encouraged extension of the territory of Judah.

But they shall swoop down on the backs of the Philistines in the
west,
together [Judah and Ephraim] they shall plunder the people
of the east.
They shall put forth their hand against Edom and Moab
and the Ammonites shall obey them (Is 11:14).

Sargon's death may have encouraged Judeans to envision their own
destiny as a great power with Egypt and Assyria:

On that day Israel will be a third with Egypt and Assyria, a
blessing in the midst of the earth (Is 21:24).

It is believable that at the time of Sargon's death Isaiah may have
written the core of the unit which came to be called the *apocalypse*.

The Destruction of a City

For you have made the city a heap,
    the fortified city a ruin:
the palace of aliens is a city no more,
    it will never be rebuilt (Is 25:2).

Some scholars see a reference to the city in all four chapters of the
unit.

The city of chaos is broken down (24:10).

For you have made the city a heap (25:2).

. . . the lofty city he lays low (26:5).

For the fortified city is solitary, a habitation deserted and
forsaken, like the wilderness (27:10).

What is the identity of the unnamed city? There has been much
scholarly speculation concerning its identity. (a) Because the unit has
been considered an *apocalypse*, many scholars have identified the city
as Babylon.[6] Those scholars who date the whole unit as originating in
the fifth century, or later, are comfortable with Babylon as the identity of the destroyed city. There are other interpretations however.

(b) The unnamed city may not be any particular city but could represent any city destroyed by Yahweh's judgment. There are no nationalistic clues to the identity of the city. This was a time of active warfare, and cities were being destroyed everywhere. When *the city* was destroyed, that nation was defeated. It was in *the city* (any capital city) that the king and leaders of the people were housed. The destroyed city (cities) would stand in contrast with the Lord's city, where the house of the Lord was located, Jerusalem. So this song would be sung in Judah:

> We have a strong city;
> > he sets up victory like walls and bulwarks.
> Open the gates, so that the righteous nation that keeps faith
> > may enter in (26:1–2).

(c) An intriguing hypothesis has been advanced by John H. Hayes and Stuart Irvine in their book, *Isaiah, the Eighth Century Prophet.*[7] Their explanation of the fortified city is that it was not a city, but a fortification in the city of Jerusalem, housing troops for the purpose of keeping Jerusalem in line with Assyrian policies. The city was:

> . . . the fortified Assyrian citadel in Jerusalem garrisoned with troops, probably from various countries, charged with the military supervision of Jerusalem and Judah. Such a citadel, comparable to the Seleucid stronghold in Jerusalem at the time of the Maccabean wars . . . was located in some elevated portion of the town.

This hypothesis fits well with references in the oracles to the city as "fortified city," "palace of strangers" and "lofty city."

A Poetic Image of Resurrection

One of the reasons why this scriptural unit has been called an apocalypse is because of a passage describing a resurrection of the dead, not dissimilar to passages in the book of Revelation (20:11–13) and in the book of Daniel (12:2). In Isaiah 26:19 we read:

> Your dead shall live, their corpses shall rise.
> > O dwellers in the dust, awake and sing for joy!

> For your dew is a radiant dew,
>   and the earth will give birth to those long dead.

There are several explanations of this passage. (a) Isaiah was concerned primarily with the fate of the nation of Israel (Judah). This passage is a bold poetic image of the resurrection of the nation of Yahweh's people. It is a metaphor of national revival. It is similar to the imagery of Ezekiel's vision of a valley of dry bones.

> Thus says the LORD God: I am going to open your graves
> and bring you up from your graves, O my people; and I will
> bring you back to the land of Israel (Ez 37:12).

God explains the meaning of the vision to Ezekiel. "Mortal, these bones are the whole house of Israel" (37:11). (b) On the other hand, if Isaiah's words are akin to the passage from Daniel:

> Many of those who sleep in the dust of the earth shall awake,
> some to everlasting life, and some to shame and everlasting
> contempt (Dan 12:2),

then the passage is a very late addition to the scroll of Isaiah, possibly as late as the second century.[8]

There is probably some truth in each explanation. It is not possible that Isaiah, a prophet of the eighth century, concerned primarily with social and political issues, could have made a statement concerning resurrection of the dead, except as a bold metaphor for national revival. However, German scholar Otto Kaiser, in a linguistic analysis of the passage, has convincingly discerned grammatical problems which reveal more than one author for the passage.[9] We believe that Isaiah's original poetic statement has been expanded under the influence of later beliefs of those who cared for and amended the scrolls.

Summary

While chapters 24 to 27 are recognized as a unit, the traditional name, The Apocalypse of Isaiah, is not entirely appropriate. There are some elements of apocalyptic literature which are not present in this section. This unit is a liturgical collection of songs and chants which may be viewed as a cantata composed for a special occasion. The occasion could have been the death of the Assyrian king, Sargon

II, in 705. The core of the unit was composed by Isaiah. Like other parts of the book containing original Isaiah material, there have been expansions by later scribes and editors.

STUDY QUESTIONS

1. In what ways does this unit (chapters 24–27) resemble apocalyptic literature?

2. What are some elements of apocalyptic literature missing in these chapters?

3. What are the circumstances leading up to our suggestion for a date for this composition?

4. In what ways do these chapters resemble a cantata?

5. Discuss three explanations as to the identity of the unnamed city.

6. What are two explanations of the passage concerning the resurrection of the dead? Which one do you favor?

NOTES

1. See for example *The New Jerome Biblical Commentary*, p. 244.

2. John F.A. Sawyer, in the *Isaiah* volume of the "The Daily Study Bible Series" (Philadelphia: Westminster, 1984), dates these four chapters to the fourth century, B.C.E. See p. 204.

3. See p. 302 of *The New Jerome Biblical Commentary*, previously cited.

4. See Peter Ackroyd's commentary "Isaiah," *The Interpreter's One-Volume Commentary*, p. 345.

5. See John Hayes and Stuart Irvine, *Isaiah, the Eighth Century Prophet* (Nashville: Abingdon, 1987), pp. 294–320.

6. In Revelation a city called Babylon plays an important, symbolic role. See Rev 14:8–18:21.

7. See pp. 296–297 of the Hayes-Irvine book, cited above, published by Abingdon Press.

8. For example see John J. Collins, *Isaiah, Collegeville Bible Commentary* (Collegeville: Liturgical Press, 1986), p. 59.

9. Otto Kaiser, *Isaiah, Chapters 13–39* (Philadelphia: Westminster, 1974), pp. 215–220.

Chapter 12

A COLLECTION OF ORACLES

Suggested Scripture Reading:

Isaiah 28–33

Following the oracles against foreign nations (13–23) and the *apocalypse* (24–27), the book of Isaiah returns to typical Isaianic prophecies such as those found in chapters 1–12. The dates for the oracles in this collection range from before the fall of Israel, 722 B.C.E., to the crisis of 701 which resulted in the invasion of Judah by Sennacherib during the reign of Hezekiah. This was a period of almost thirty years. We have discovered three collections of oracles in our review of Isaiah of Jerusalem:

Early Oracles	Chapters 1–12
Oracles Against Nations	Chapters 13–23
Assorted Oracles	Chapters 28–33

Since the final editing of this last collection of oracles took place after the Babylonian captivity (late sixth century), there are editorial comments from several redactional hands.

In our examination of the collection of oracles found at the beginning of the book of Isaiah, chapters 1–12, we were able to identify a prelude, or introduction (chapter 1), a concluding Psalm (chapter 12), and a core around which the oracles were arranged, the memoirs of Isaiah (6:1–8:18). In this collection we find that the oracles have been arranged by an editor so that words of hope and words of judgment alternate with each other. This alternation (of words of hope with words of judgment) can be seen clearly in the following oracles:

108

PATTERN OF ALTERNATING *WORDS OF JUDGMENT* AND *WORDS OF HOPE* IN ISAIAH 28–33

Ariel, City of David (29:1–4) Part One	judgment
Ariel, City of David (29:5–8) Part Two	hope
Stupefy yourselves (29:9–16)	judgment
Good news for Lebanon and Jacob (29:17–24)	hope
Rebellious children (30:1–17)	judgment
The Lord waits to be gracious (30:18–26)	hope
Bad news for Assyria (30:27–28)	judgment
A song in the night (30:29–33)	hope
Alas for those who look to Egypt (31:1–3)	judgment
Protection for Jerusalem (31:6–32:8)	hope
Complacent women who are at ease (32:9–15)	judgment
Justice in the wilderness (32:16–20)	hope

It is important in reading this collection to remember that it is a *collection* from different times in the prophetic ministry of Isaiah, and for this reason there is no logical development as such. The first three oracles in the collection give us a good illustration of how some oracles are located in prophetic clusters. Read the first verse of each of the first three oracles.

(1) Ah, the proud garland of the drunkards of Ephraim (Is 28:1).

(2) In that day the Lord of Hosts will be a garland of glory (Is 28:5).

(3) These also reel with wine and stagger with strong drink (Is 28:7).

AN EXAMPLE OF CHIASM IN ISAIAH 28

Chiasm is a literary structure found frequently in the Hebrew Bible. The term chiasm comes from the Greek letter Chi (χ) because the top of the letter is a mirror image of the bottom (and the left is a mirror image of the right). In a chiastic structure, the completion of 123 would be 321. A chiastic structure is not always obvious in English, but in chapter 28 we have a good example. The passage starts out with a reference to the alliance with Egypt of 705 as a covenant with death. The word death is used in the opening (and closing) oracle in two ways. First, this alliance will lead to death, and, second, it is with Egypt, a land preoccupied with death. Next comes a figure of a storm which will do tremendous damage, from which there will be a need of refuge and shelter. The third figure is an architectural figure of a testing stone. Last, there is the quotation, "One who trusts will not panic." Following the quotation the three figures are repeated in reverse order:

A	Covenant with death	v. 15a
B	Damaging storm	v. 15b
C	Architectural figure	v. 16a
D	Quotation	v. 16b
C	Architectural figure	v. 17a
B	Damaging storm	v. 17b
A	Covenant with death	v. 18

The first thing we notice is the alternating pattern: judgment, hope, judgment. These three oracles[1] may have no close connection with each other and may have originated at different times in Isaiah's ministry. They appear consecutively because of what has been called the "catchword" principle, which is an editorial principle for the physical location of otherwise unattached oracles. The word "garland" in the opening sentence of the second oracle matches the same word in verse one of the first oracle. The mention of drunkards of Ephraim influences the placement of the third oracle which starts with a reference to priests and prophets who "reel with wine and stagger with strong drink."

We will discuss several of the oracles of the collection and comment on several others.

Military Alliances with Foreign Nations

Both Isaiah and Hosea were opposed to military or political alliances with foreign powers. It comes as a surprise to many students that these eighth century prophets were more concerned with foreign political alliances than they were with cultic purity. In the original oracles of the eighth century prophets we find that they had less to say about idolatry than political alliances and economic conditions.

For one thing, the oracles of Hosea and Isaiah were chiefly addressed to the decision makers of Samaria and Jerusalem and not to the people at large. These decision makers were the ones who were able to make alliances with foreign military powers for the protection and survival of the nation. Both Hosea and Isaiah were angry with the leaders of Israel and Judah. By looking to Egypt or Assyria for deliverance these decision makers were abandoning and rejecting Yahweh and destroying an ancient living relationship with the God of Israel's youth. We should note the use of words refuge and shelter in the following verse:

> . . . to take refuge in the protection of Pharaoh
>   and to seek shelter in the shadow of Egypt (30:2).

These terms, and similar terms, are used to describe Judah's relationship with her God throughout the Psalms.[2] Their use here, applied to Egypt, is significant.

In Hosea the language which addresses this issue is poetic, based on several metaphors, including one of infidelity:

> Ephraim is like a dove, silly and without sense,
>   calling to Egypt, going to Assyria.
> As they go I will spread my net over them;
>   I will bring them down like birds of the air (Hos 7:11–12).

> Ephraim has hired lovers.
>   Though they hire allies from among the nations,
>   I will soon gather them up (Hos 8:9–10).

> . . . they make a treaty with Assyria
>   and oil is carried to Egypt (Hos 12:1).

While Hosea and Isaiah shared a strong message of condemnation for the activity which produced foreign alliances for military protection,

replacing reliance on Yahweh as Israel's sole rescuer, the oracles of
Isaiah are stronger and more explicit. Two of these oracles appear in
the collection found in chapters 28–33.

> O rebellious children, says the LORD,
>   who carry out a plan, but not mine;
> who make an alliance, but against my will,
>   adding sin to sin:
> who set out to go down to Egypt without asking my counsel,
>   to take refuge in the protection of Pharaoh,
>   to seek shelter in the shadow of Egypt;
> Therefore the protection of Pharaoh shall become your shame,
>   and the shelter in the shadow of Egypt your humiliation
>   (Is 30:1–3).

> Alas for those who go down to Egypt for help
>   and who rely on horses,
> who trust in chariots because they are many
>   and in horsemen because they are very strong,
> but do not look to the Holy One of Israel
>   or consult the LORD! (Is 31:1).

A military alliance with a foreign power for protection, whether
it was with Assyria for protection against Israel/Syria, or with Egypt
for protection against Assyria, was considered by Isaiah as a rejection
of Yahweh and a lack of faith. The leaders did not look to the Holy
One of Israel. It was he who would protect his people:

> Like birds hovering overhead,
>   so the LORD of hosts will protect Jerusalem:
> He will protect and deliver it,
>   he will spare and rescue it (Is 31:5).

In a stirring oracle beginning with the words "Ah, Ariel, Ariel,
the city where David encamped!" (Is 29:1), we have a description of
Yahweh's fight to save the city and his people:

> But the multitude of your foes shall be like small dust,
>   and the multitude of tyrants like flying chaff.
> And in an instant, suddenly, you will be visited by the LORD of
>   hosts
>   with thunder and earthquake and great noise,

with whirlwind and tempest, and the flame of a devouring fire.
And the multitude of all the nations that fight against Ariel,
   all that fight against her and her stronghold, and who distress
      her,
shall be like a dream, a vision of the night (Is 29:5-7).

Isaiah and Wisdom Literature

For the bed is too short to stretch oneself on it, and the
covering is too narrow to wrap oneself in it (Is 28:20).

The above words are a proverbial saying. Proverbs are found in
many cultures, and Judah had a strong wisdom tradition where proverbs were valued and enjoyed. A modern parallel to the above prov-
erb might be, "I'm always a day late and a dollar short."

Wisdom literature consists of more than proverbs, however.
There are essays, or wise descriptions of various aspects of life and the
business of living. There are interesting questions and clever answers,
and poetic comparisons. Parallelism is the chief form used in wisdom
literature.

Wisdom literature in the Hebrew Bible is interesting because it is
often secular in nature. As many parts of the book of Proverbs demonstrate, there is no need to mention Yahweh, salvation history, or cultic
practices.

Parts of the eighth century prophetic books are composed of
wisdom literature. There is a dispute among scholars as to whether
Amos and Isaiah wrote wisdom passages themselves, to present their
oracles in a "wisdom" setting, or whether the wisdom passages were
the work of redactors and editors who valued wisdom and saw a place
for it in the prophetic books. In the collection of oracles we are examining there are several wisdom passages. For example:

Do those who plow for sowing plow continually?
   Do they continually open and harrow their ground?
When they have leveled its surface, do they not scatter dill, sow
      cummin,
   and plant wheat in rows and barley in its proper place, and
      spelt as the border?
For they are well instructed; their God teaches them
   (Is 28:24-26).[3]

In this paragraph, and the one which follows (28:27–29), the author is saying that different times require different actions by a farmer, the same actors change their roles (from plowing to sowing to harvesting), that different seeds require different handling, things are done one step at a time, and so forth. The implication is that Yahweh is wise. He disciplines when it is the right time and heals when it is appropriate. Or it could be applied to Assyria, the rod in God's hands. Assyria is allowed to be destructive at one time, when it is right in God's wisdom, but later God will punish Assyria and bring her low as punishment for her pride. God is like the wise farmer who does different things at different times to produce a desired result as time passes.

Another wisdom passage is found in chapter 32:1–8, ending with these words:

The villainies of villains are evil;
    they devise wicked devices to ruin the poor with lying words,
    even when the plea of the needy is right.
But those who are noble plan noble things,
    and by noble things they stand (Is 32:7–8).

In a prophetic ministry which lasted forty years it is possible that Isaiah had a period when he utilized this type of wisdom genre. Many scholars attribute this passage about the farmer to Isaiah. Our guess, however, is that these are not the words of Isaiah, but are the words of a redactor who valued wisdom and wanted to raise it above its secular role in Judah and demonstrate its value in expounding, expanding, and promoting the truth contained in Isaiah's prophetic oracles.

The Earliest Form of Faith as a Religious Concept

For thus said the LORD God, the Holy One of Israel:
In returning and rest you shall be saved;
    in quietness and in trust shall be your strength (30:15).

The concept of faith and trust in God is so basic to our current understanding of religion that it is difficult for the modern student to imagine a time when faith was not the sole foundation of religious experience. It may come as a surprise that, historically, the first concrete expressions of faith and trust are found in the eighth century oracles of Isaiah, and, further, that these concepts grew out of Isaiah's reaction to the military threat of enemy invasion of Jerusalem.

For Isaiah, faith in Yahweh meant trusting in Yahweh's power to save Jerusalem. Trusting in anything else was expressly forbidden. This included the military power of foreign nations (Egypt, Syria, or Assyria), military power of any type (horses and chariots), and any gods other than Yahweh. There are many passages in Isaiah which summarize these concrete views. For example, in criticizing a proposed alliance with Egypt mentioned above (Is 30:1–3), Isaiah explained:

> The Egyptians are human, and not God;
> their horses are flesh, and not spirit (31:3).

In this example, an alliance with Egypt was denounced as a betrayal of Yahweh, an abandonment of Judah's long-standing relationship with Yahweh as Israel's sole savior. Earlier, when Ahaz was urged to make an alliance with the anti-Assyrian coalition of Syria and Israel, Isaiah told Ahaz to have faith only in Yahweh:

> Take heed, be quiet, do not fear,
> and do not let your heart be faint . . . (7:4).

The essence of Isaiah's concept of trust and faith is found in Psalm 46:

> Come, behold the works of the LORD . . .
> he breaks the bow, and shatters the spear;
> he burns the shields with fire.
> Be still, and know that I am God!

In the conclusion of Isaiah's words to Ahaz, warning him against caving in to the alliance with Syria and Israel, Isaiah told Ahaz that he must have faith in Yahweh.

> If you do not stand firm in faith,
> you shall not stand at all (7:9).

The Hebrew word for stand firm is the same word for believe (*ta'aminu*), and the root *'mn* is the root of the word amen, a Hebrew, and English, response signifying "I believe."

Our statement that it is in the oracles of Isaiah that faith and trust make their first appearance in the Hebrew Bible[4] is supported by a lack of these concepts in the oracles of the other eighth century prophets. There is no counterpart in Amos or Micah. While it is true that, in the original oracles of Hosea, foreign alliances were severely condemned, and declared to be a betrayal of Yahweh, there are no corresponding exhortations to believe, or to have faith, nor are there statements of assurance like Isaiah's words:

> In returning and rest you shall be saved;
>   in quietness and in trust shall be your strength (Is 30:15).

The Inviolability of Jerusalem

It is in one of the oracles in this collection that a clear statement is made describing a concept which scholars have called "The Inviolability of Jerusalem."

> . . . the LORD of hosts will come down
>   to fight upon Mount Zion and upon its hill.
> Like birds hovering overhead,
>   so the LORD of hosts will protect Jerusalem;
> he will protect it and deliver it,
>   he will spare it and rescue it (Is 31:4–5).

The belief that Jerusalem was a special place which could not be destroyed by her enemies has many roots in ancient Israel. We have previously mentioned that even before the acquisition of Jerusalem by David there was a belief that Mount Zion was the mountain of God (Zion theology), the home of El, the high god of the Canaanites and Jebusites. The Davidic theology added another layer of belief regarding Jerusalem. Yahweh promised David an eternal house; Jerusalem was its location. Some theologians believe that it was in Jerusalem that Yahweh and El became merged as one God.[5]

In summary, these are some of the factors which caused many ancient citizens of Jerusalem to believe that the city could not be destroyed:

(a) Zion theology;
(b) Davidic theology;
(c) the belief that Yahweh had chosen Jerusalem as his home;
(d) the failure of the Syro-Ephraimitic coalition to come against Jerusalem in the days of Ahaz;

(e) the failure of Sennacherib to destroy the city after capturing and destroying forty-six cities and towns of Judah.

The scripture passage above (31:4–5) and other similar passages are believed to be reflections of a belief that Jerusalem could not be destroyed. When the city of Jerusalem was finally destroyed by the Babylonians in 587, this superficial belief, along with many other misconceptions concerning Yahweh and his people, had to be re-thought, revised, and otherwise updated. We will be able to touch on this process in our chapter 15 when we discuss the writings of Deutero-Isaiah.

STUDY QUESTIONS

1. We have discovered three collections of oracles in Isaiah. In what chapters are they located? How many years are covered by the last collection?

2. Explain the pattern of alternation for the arrangement of oracles which we have pointed out in this chapter.

3. What is the catchword principle?

4. What is the difference between Isaiah's oracles against foreign alliances and Hosea's? Give an example.

5. What are some characteristics of wisdom literature? Is it possible that Isaiah wrote wisdom? Is it probable? Give your opinion.

6. What was the primary audience addressed by the oracles of Isaiah?

7. Explain Isaiah's concept of faith.

8. What do we mean by the inviolability of Jerusalem? What are some of the factors contributing to this belief?

NOTES

1. The second oracle of these three may be a short oracle or a fragment of a longer oracle which an editor wanted to include in the collection (28:5–6).

2. See Psalms 27, 46, 121 for examples.

3. For a complete study of agriculture in ancient Israel consult David C. Hopkin's study, *The Highlands of Canaan* (Sheffield: JSOT Press, 1985).

4. The student may feel that the patriarchs (Abraham and Jacob) and the early champions and leaders of Israel (Moses and Joshua) surely had *faith* in Yahweh. This is a very complicated subject. The canonical versions of the books of the Pentateuch and the historical books contain many passages which could be used as examples of faith in Yahweh. What we are saying is that in Isaiah we have the earliest (eighth century) written examples of a primitive, foundational, form of faith, and that this concept is an objective, theological concept. Most of the books which appear in the Hebrew Bible, reporting earlier times, did not reach their canonical form until after the eighth century. Many statements which could be described as examples of faith were projections into the past of understandings developed after the days of Isaiah.

Much later, in the first century, when concepts of faith were mature and reached their ultimate expression, the author of the book of Hebrews in the Christian scriptures could interpret everything that Abraham did as acts of faith. Read Hebrews 11:8–22.

5. It is a very complicated matter to review the relationship between Yahweh, the savior God of Israel, and El, a god of the Canaanites. There was no *one* theology of Israel or *one* perception of Yahweh before the last days of the captivity and the days of the restoration of Jerusalem which followed. During most of the history of Israel there were many viewpoints, separated by geography, and in some cases there were several theological viewpoints in the same location. For example, in the days of King Josiah there were two distinct theological views, promoted by two priesthoods, which hardly agreed on any basic issue. For this reason, in the context of this book, we cannot explore in depth the issues connected with the sacredness of Jerusalem and the inviolability of the city. It is important enough in our opinion, however, to bring the subject to the student's attention.

Chapter 13

JUDGMENT AND SALVATION

Suggested Scripture Reading:

Isaiah 34–35

It is generally agreed that all the oracles of Isaiah of Jerusalem are located in the first thirty-three chapters of the book. Chapters 34 and 35 of Isaiah, which we now review, are recognized as a unit composed late in the period of the Babylonian exile, or even later, during the period of the rebuilding of Jerusalem.[1] It is frequently called the Little Apocalypse of Isaiah because it starts with a statement concerning the destruction of the world, has a cosmic dimension, and ends with a stirring proclamation of a new age for the people of Judah. Although it is beyond the scope of this book to illustrate it, the two chapters share "a coherence of vocabulary and style."[2]

Chapter 34 is a statement of judgment, and chapter 35 a statement of hope. By this time we are very familiar with the alternation of these two themes.

Judgment for the Nations, Especially Edom

Chapter 34 opens with a brutal description of destruction to be visited on the nations of the earth because Yahweh is furious with them (vv. 1–4). The reason for his fury is not given. In verse 5 his wrath is directed to Edom. This raises several questions. Was this chapter originally directed to Edom, a brother nation located immediately to Judah's south, then expanded to include the opening statement addressed to the nations? Or was the mention of Edom intended

119

to supply a detailed illustration of the terrible things which will happen to the nations on the day of Yahweh's wrath? There is an interesting parallel in the book of Ezekiel where two chapters (35 and 36) sit side by side, one condemning Edom and the nations, and the next proclaiming a day of blessing for Israel.

> Therefore thus saith the LORD God: I am speaking in my hot jealousy *against the rest of the nations and against Edom,* who with wholehearted joy and utter contempt took my land as their possession, because of its pasture, to plunder it (Ez 36:5).

It is believed that during the tragedy of 587, when the Babylonians destroyed the temple of Jerusalem and leveled the walls of the city, ending the history of Judah as an independent political entity, Edom took advantage of Judah's defeat by expanding its own territory. In a short oracle against Edom found in Amos, but dated from the period of captivity, there is an indication that Edom ruthlessly participated in the attack on Judah instead of offering support.

> . . . he [Edom] pursued his brother with the sword and cast off all pity (Am 1:11).

Edom was called *brother* because of a tradition that the Edomites were descended from Esau, the brother of Jacob:

> So Esau settled in the hill country of Seir; Esau is Edom (Gen 36:8).

Edom pursued his brother with the sword; now the sword of Yahweh will be turned on Edom:

> When my sword has drunk its fill in the heavens,
>   lo, it will descend upon Edom,
>   upon the people I have doomed to judgment (34:5).

This chapter is a revelation of intense bitter feelings directed against Edom. The land will be cursed like Sodom; volcanic imagery is employed:

PARALLEL IMAGES FROM SECOND ISAIAH
FOUND IN CHAPTER 35

Chapter 35	Second Isaiah
Opening the eyes of the blind (v. 5)	43:20
Streams in the desert (v. 6)	43:19, 44:3
A highway in the desert (v. 8)	40:3 and 49:11
Returnees are called "redeemed" (v. 9)	44:22
And the ransomed of the LORD shall return, and come to Zion with singing . . . (v. 10) (Closing paragraph of chapter 35 is found in 51:11)	51:11

> And the streams of Edom shall be turned into pitch
> and her soil into sulfur;
> her land shall become burning pitch.
> Night and day it shall not be quenched;
> its smoke shall go up forever (34:9–10).

Where life is possible in this cursed land, the only animals to be found are mysterious animals who do not live where humans dwell, including Lilith (v. 14), a mythological (Mesopotamian) female demon of the night who is mentioned in the Talmud. The mention of wild animals and demons which will inhabit the land is related in the oracle against Babylon found in Isaiah 13:

> But wild animals will lie down there,
> and its houses will be full of howling creatures;
> there ostriches will live,
> and there goat-demons will dance (Is 13:21).

The horror of chapter 34 stands in stark contrast with the hope and joy of chapter 35 and intensifies its impact.

Hope and Joy for the People of Yahweh

The wilderness and the dry land shall be glad,
    the desert shall rejoice and blossom (35:1).

This chapter previews for us joyous themes of Second Isaiah
(chapters 40–55) which proclaim the end of captivity and the return
home for the people of Yahweh. Scholars have noted the influence of
Second Isaiah on this chapter. As God's people return home the desert will blossom like a garden, miraculously watered by Yahweh.

    For waters shall break forth in the wilderness,
        and streams in the desert;
    the burning sand shall become a pool,
        and the thirsty ground springs of water (35:6–7).

To make the long journey home safe, Yahweh will provide a highway
through the wilderness for his people:

    . . . it shall be for God's people;
        no traveler, not even fools shall go astray.
    No lion shall be there,
        nor shall any ravenous beast come up on it;
    they shall not be found there
        but the redeemed shall walk there (35:8–9).

While the Judahites were in Babylon they observed processional
walks between the temples and sacred places of Babylonian worship.
Some scholars have seen the influence of these "holy ways" in this
passage. There is no doubt concerning the appropriateness of this
liturgical hymn for processions in the rebuilt temple of Jerusalem
following the captivity.

    It is possible that at one time in the development of the book of
Isaiah, chapter 35 may have been next to our present chapter 40. If it
was separated from chapter 40 to make room for the insertion of the
historical narrative concerning Isaiah and Hezekiah, then it obtained
a life of its own as a beautiful example of a changed world seen
through the eyes of faith.

    The face of all the world is changed
        since first I heard the footsteps of thy soul.

The road home as seen through the eyes of captives would be
transformed.

The glory of Lebanon shall be given it,
   the majesty of Carmel and Sharon.
They shall see the glory of the LORD,
   the majesty of our God (35:2).

Under the influence of Zion theology, returning to Jerusalem meant returning to Yahweh. This geographic journey would have profound theological implications. The concept of returning to Yahweh would be projected back into the prophetic books of the eighth century prophets to an extent which they may not have been able to express or conceive.

STUDY QUESTIONS

1. Why is the unit consisting of chapters 34 and 35 sometimes called the Little Apocalypse of Isaiah?

2. What was the relationship of Judah to Edom according to tradition?

3. Why did Judahites have such hard feelings against Edomites?

4. In what ways can chapter 35 be considered parallel to the oracles of Second Isaiah?

5. In what sense may the return to Jerusalem and the concept of repentance be related?

NOTES

1. John L. McKenzie begins his Anchor Bible Series commentary *Second Isaiah* (New York: Doubleday, 1983) by translating and commenting on chapters 34 and 35. He includes chapter 35 because of the sameness of spirit and style as Second Isaiah. He includes chapter 34, with its harsh judgment, because he recognizes it as part of a unit with chapter 35. Note: although Father McKenzie's book is entitled *Second Isaiah*, it also includes translation and commentary on Isaiah chapters 56–66, a section usually called by scholars Third Isaiah.

2. R.E. Clements, *Isaiah 1–39*, p. 34.

Chapter 14

HISTORICAL NARRATIVES OF ISAIAH AND HEZEKIAH

Suggested Scripture Reading:

Isaiah 36–39

After working our way through thirty-five chapters of prophetic oracles, the historical narratives of chapters 36 to 39 come as a most welcome change of pace. On one level they are easy to understand. On another level, however, they are easy to misunderstand. For one thing, although we call them *historical*, they are not strictly objective reports of factual information, as modern history strives to be. As history they are more like the "histories" of Shakespeare, similar to Richard III or Henry V, which tell us more about Elizabethan England than the days in which the events were believed to have occurred. These Isaianic narratives tell us more about the days of Josiah than the days of Hezekiah.

This collection came together almost a century after the events they record, during the period of Josiah and the days of the formation of the Deuteronomistic History (DH). So we are not surprised to find these four chapters appearing almost word for word in DH (2 Kgs 18:13–20:19). Some scholars believe that DH copied the events as reported from the scroll of Isaiah, and some scholars think that Isaiah (the scroll) incorporated the material from DH.[1]

But there are differences in the two sections. We will list the differences from the viewpoint of the book of Isaiah.

(1) There is no report in Isaiah of Hezekiah paying a large amount of tribute to Sennacherib. In DH we read:

SENNACHERIB'S ATTACK ON JERUSALEM IN 701

The Assyrian record of Sennacherib's attack on Jerusalem in 701 was discovered on a six-sided prism in Nineveh by Colonel R. Taylor in 1830. The account agrees substantially with the biblical account in Isaiah and Kings. In the Assyrian account, the amount of tribute is greater than that reported in the Bible. The prism is now located in the British Museum.

As for Hezekiah of Judah, he did not submit to my yoke, and I laid siege to forty-six of his strong cities, walled forts, and to the countless small villages in their vicinity, and conquered them using earth ramps and battering rams. These siege engines were aided by the use of foot soldiers who undermined the walls. I drove out of these places 200,150 people—young and old, male and female, horses, mules, donkeys, camels, large and small cattle beyond counting and considered them as booty. I made Hezekiah a prisoner in Jerusalem, like a bird in a cage. I erected siege works to prevent anyone escaping through the city gates. The towns in his territory which I captured I gave to Mitini, King of Ashdod, Padi, King of Ekron, and Sillibel, King of Gaza. Thus I reduced his territory in this campaign, and I also increased Hezekiah's annual tribute payments.

Hezekiah, who was overwhelmed by my terror-inspiring splendor, was deserted by his elite troops, which he had brought into Jerusalem, and was forced to send me thirty talents of gold, eight hundred talents of silver, precious stones, couches and chairs inlaid with ivory, elephant hides, ebony wood, box wood, and all kinds of valuable treasures, his daughters, concubines, and male and female musicians. He sent his personal messenger to deliver this tribute and bow down to me.

2 Kings 18

Now in the fourteenth year of Hezekiah, Sennacherib, king of Assyria, attacked all the strongholds of Judah and took them (18:13).

Then Hezekiah, king of Judah, sent messengers to the king of Assyria at Lachish, bidding them to say to him: "I have sinned; cease from attacking me. Everything you put on me I will submit to it." The king of Assyria caused Hezekiah king of Judah, to pay three hundred talents of silver and thirty talents of gold (18:14).

Hezekiah gave him all the silver that was found in the house of Yahweh and in the storehouse of the king's palace (18:15).

At that time Hezekiah stripped (of their plating) the doors of the sanctuary of Yahweh, as well as the pillars which . . . the king of Judah had covered [with metal] and he sent it all to the king of Assyria (18:16).

Hezekiah gave him [Sennacherib] all the silver that was found in the house of the LORD and in the treasuries of the king's house. At that time Hezekiah stripped the gold from the doors of the temple of the LORD, and from the doorpost that King Hezekiah of Judah had overlaid and gave it to the king of Assyria (2 Kgs 18:15–16).

This account of recapitulation to Sennacherib does not appear in Isaiah.

(2) There is a psalm of Hezekiah in Isaiah (Is 38:9–20) which does not appear in DH.

(3) In Isaiah, Hezekiah does not specifically inquire as to the nature of the sign as he does in DH.

Hezekiah said to Isaiah, "What shall be the sign that the LORD will heal me" (2 Kgs 20:8)?

As we analyze these narratives we should first note that there are three events, and the three need not be connected. The three are:

(a) The siege of Jerusalem and the speech against Jerusalem by the Rabshakeh.

(b) Hezekiah's illness and recovery.

(c) The visit of the Babylonian envoys to Jerusalem.

The three events are not in correct chronological order. The visit of the Babylonian envoys was probably the earliest event. It took place between 721 and 710 when Merodach-baladan (Marduk-apal-iddina), occupied the throne of the city-state of Babylon.[2]

The Babylonian Envoys

We know why the event of the visit of the envoys was placed last in the narrative grouping. By being last, it would serve as a bridge between First Isaiah and Second Isaiah. Second Isaiah is concerned with the people of Yahweh in Babylonian captivity, and this visit, including Isaiah's response, shifts the focus from Assyria to Babylon because of Isaiah's prediction (39:6).

The content of Isaiah's prediction assists us in identifying the date of the composition.

Days are coming when all that is in your house, and that which your ancestors have stored up until this day, shall be

carried to Babylon; nothing shall be left, says the LORD
(Is 39:6).

In the early sixth century, a century after the reign of Hezekiah, the
Babylonians plundered Jerusalem twice, in 597 and in 587. For ten
years Jerusalem and the temple were spared, offering an opportunity
for the Judahites to be obedient and profitable vassals to Babylon. In
587 Nebuchadnezzar lost patience with Judah and made a decision to
destroy Jerusalem.

> And they burned the house of God, and broke down the wall
> of Jerusalem, and burned all its palaces with fire, and de-
> stroyed all its precious vessels (2 Chr 36:19).

Since the dire prediction attributed to Isaiah makes no mention of the
destruction of the temple or the breaking down of the walls, but
mentions as the worst affliction the carrying away of treasure, it is
logical to believe that the account was composed after the first invasion of Jerusalem by Babylon, 597, but before the final invasion
in 587.

Deuteronomistic Characteristics of This Account

If the account of the visiting envoys from Babylon was finalized
between 597 and 587 as we have suggested, we would expect to find
signs of the Deuteronomist viewpoint. There are several. (a) Isaiah is
called by the title *nabi* (39:3).[3] This was the favorite title for a prophet
in the Deuteronomic History. However in the first thirty-five
chapters of Isaiah he is never called or referred to by the use of the
word *nabi*. Only in the four narrative chapters (36–39) is Isaiah called
a *nabi*. (b) Isaiah tells of the day when the Babylonians will carry away
the treasures of Jerusalem (39:6). One of the characteristics of DH is
the prophecy-fulfillment scheme.[4] There are dozens of examples of
prophets telling in advance what will happen in Israel and Judah. This
is summed up in an oracle appearing in Amos 3:7.

> Surely the LORD does nothing without revealing his secret
> to his servants the prophets (*nabiim*).

Why the Envoys Were in Jerusalem

During the time that Merodach-baladan was in Babylon, 721–
710, there was a Philistine rebellion against Assyria, called the Ash-

dod rebellion. Merodach-baladan would have profited from this rebellion in the Palestine area. Although it is only speculation, it is
possible that Merodach-baladan sent envoys to encourage Yamani of
Ashdod-by-the-Sea in the anti-Assyrian rebellion (714), and during
the same trip the envoys stopped in Jerusalem to enlist the aid of
Hezekiah.

This would supply the provocation for the hostile prophecy of
Isaiah who would see, in Hezekiah's openness to the envoys, movement toward participation in yet another anti-Assyrian coalition
which Isaiah opposed. The author of this event opens it by stating that
the envoys were sent to Jerusalem because Merodach-baladan had
heard that Hezekiah had been sick. This is highly unlikely. The author, living in the late seventh century, may not have known about the
Ashdod rebellion.

In closing our review of this event we note that although Hezekiah appealed to Yahweh during the siege of Jerusalem by Sennacherib, and at the time of his illness, he did not appeal to Yahweh in this
incident. Some scholars believe that this fatalism may have been typical of the last decade of Judah's existence, the time which we have
assigned for the composition of this event, 597–587, when the Bible
history reports no appeal to Yahweh by Zedekiah to save Jerusalem.

Hezekiah's Illness

The account of Hezekiah's illness has folkloristic elements. The
shadow cast by the declining sun reverses itself on the steps of the dial
of Ahaz. Some scholars state that the steps referred to were not originally meant to serve as a sun dial, but were used as an indication of the
time of day because of the shadow cast by the afternoon sun.

The psalm of Hezekiah is beautiful, filled with poetic imagery.
There is nothing in the psalm to identify Hezekiah specifically. The
role of Isaiah in the healing does not add to our picture of the historic
person of Isaiah.

The Siege of Jerusalem by Sennacherib

The last event, chronologically, of the narrative section (chapters
36–39) is a fitting event to close our review of First Isaiah. It is fitting
for many reasons, as it primarily involves (a) the house of David, (b)
the pride of the Assyrians, (c) the inviolability of Jerusalem, (d) the

futility of trusting in Egypt, (e) and the meaning of faith—trusting in Yahweh for deliverance—all theological themes of First Isaiah. This event is broken down into six parts:

(a) The speech of the Rabshakeh (36:1–22)
(b) Isaiah informed by Hezekiah (37:1–7)
(c) Further threats to Jerusalem by letter (37:8–13)
(d) Hezekiah's prayer for deliverance of Jerusalem (37:13–20)
(e) Yahweh's message to Hezekiah through Isaiah (37:21–35)
(f) Defeat of Assyrians; death of Sennacherib (37:36–38)

The Speech of Rabshakeh

Do we have an actual speech of a representative of Sennacherib, or do we have a theological reconstruction? Although some scholars point out that Assyrian speeches of negotiation were very much like the speech of the Rabshakeh, we offer another explanation. What we have in 36:4–20 is a theological reconstruction written by someone who was familiar with the recorded boastings of the Assyrians. There are at least three reasons for our conclusion. First, who was there to take notes when the Rabshakeh made his speech? Second, this account was put together a century after the events described. Third, there is too much Isaianic theology in the Rabshakeh's speech.

Isaiah had stressed the necessity of trusting in Yahweh, not on an alliance with Egypt (32:7, 31:3), or in horses and chariots (31:1). Like the passage in chapter 10:5, Assyria is recognized as a rod in the hand of Yahweh. The boastfulness of the speech reflects the words of Isaiah 10:12–14.

> I have removed the boundaries of peoples, and have plundered
>   their treasures;
>   like a bull I have brought down those who sat on thrones
>   (10:13).

The closing of the speech is meant not only to embarrass the Rabshakeh and glorify Yahweh, but to highlight the main point of the story, that faith in Yahweh is the reason for the deliverance of Jerusalem. The author, knowing that Jerusalem was delivered, has the Assyrian say:

Where are the gods of Sepharvaim?

Have they delivered Samaria out of my hand?
Who among the gods of these countries have saved their
     countries out of my hand,
   that the LORD [Yahweh] should save Jerusalem out of my
     hand (36:20)?

Two Traditions Combined

A careful reading of the text reveals that two traditions concerning this event were combined to produce the present story.[5] In one
tradition the Rabshakeh makes a speech at the upper pool on the
highway to the fuller's field. This is the same place where Isaiah met
Ahaz during the Syro-Ephraimitic crisis. In the second tradition a
letter is sent to Hezekiah containing the threat from Assyria to Jerusalem. In one tradition Isaiah responds with a short message of
assurance:

Do not be afraid because of the words which you have
heard. . . . I myself will put a spirit in him, so that he shall
hear a rumor, and return to his own land; I will cause him to
fall by the sword in his own land (37:7).

In the second tradition, there is a long response from Isaiah consisting
of a poetic oracle and a prose conclusion, ending with the words:

By the way that he came, by the same he shall return; he shall
not come into this city, says the LORD. For I will defend the
city to save it, for my own sake and for the sake of my servant
David (37:34–35).

The legend concerning the slaying of the Assyrians by the angel of the
Lord was not part of either tradition, but was known in ancient Egypt
and Greece. It was added to the merged edition of the two original
traditions.

Summary

The narratives of Hezekiah and Isaiah were composed, basically,
during the final decades of Judah's existence as a political entity.
Because of this, and also because of the period which they describe—
the closing years of Isaiah's prophetic activity—they form the ideal

conclusion to the first section of the book of Isaiah. As we stated in our introduction, it would be comfortable for the student if we could say that chapters 1 to 39 were completed before the Babylonian exile, before Deutero-Isaiah (chapters 40–55) and Trito-Isaiah (chapters 56–66). However, as we have discovered in our review of Isaiah 1–39, exilic (and perhaps some post-exilic) editorial activity is present throughout. Some sections, such as chapters 34 and 35, are completely exilic. Other sections, such as the oracles which mention foreign nations (13–23) and the *apocalypse* (24–27), are heavily redacted.

For this reason it will be profitable to move to a broad review of Second Isaiah and Third Isaiah and their relationship to the first thirty-nine chapters.

STUDY QUESTIONS

1. What are the three events appearing in the narrative section (chapters 36–39)? Which event came last chronologically?

2. Why is the chronology of the three events rearranged?

3. How do we determine the date when the account of the visit of the Babylonian envoys was written? What did Isaiah predict?

4. What political developments would have placed the Babylonian envoys in the area of Judah?

5. In conjunction with Isaiah's harsh prediction after the visit of the envoys, Hezekiah does not appeal to Yahweh for deliverance. What may this lack of appeal reflect?

6. Why is the event of the siege of Jerusalem theologically significant to close a review of First Isaiah?

7. Why do we think that the speech of the Rabshakeh is a theological reconstruction?

NOTES

1. R.E. Clements says that the setting of the material in DH is original (*Isaiah 1–39*, p. 277), but Hayes and Irvine, in *Isaiah, the Eighth Century Prophet*, p. 372, are equally sure that the original

setting is the scroll of Isaiah. The arrangement of the chronology of the events to allow the "delegation from Babylon incident" to serve as a bridge between the Assyrian period and the Babylonian period supports this latter opinion.

2. Merodach-baladan took over the city-state of Babylon in 721 during the reign of the Assyrian king Sargon II. This would be at the time that Samaria was destroyed and the kingdom of Israel was defeated by Shalmaneser, followed by Sargon II. Ten years later, in 710, Merodach-baladan was chased from Babylon by the Assyrians. He returned to Babylon again in 703 and stayed for less than a year. If the visit of the Babylonian envoys took place in 703, it would still have happened before the invasion of Judah and the siege of Jerusalem in 701 by Sennacherib.

3. Nowhere in the first thirty-five chapters is the Hebrew word *nabi* applied to Isaiah. However in chapter 8:3 Isaiah is reported to have called his wife *the prophetess*, using the feminine form of the word *nabi*.

4. Consult the chart in *Reading the Old Testament*, by Lawrence Boadt, pp. 379–380, for examples of the prophecy-fulfillment scheme.

5. In many accounts of the Hebrew Bible we have a combination of two or more traditions. During the oral stage, there were local traditions of well-known events. Sometimes these local traditions would develop and grow in different directions. When the Bible history was committed to writing, disparate accounts were skillfully combined to use both traditions. This can be seen in many places, including two accounts of creation, two flood stories, two reasons given for the fleeing of Jacob to Mesopotamia, two sets of plagues in Egypt, two accounts of Saul's hostility to David, and so forth. In some cases these traditions were divided north and south. In other cases there were more than two traditions to merge. It is not easy to disentangle these divergent accounts. In the end the theology of the story would determine its content rather than an understanding of historical fact. This type of literature is sometimes called narrative theology.

Chapter 15

THE MAJESTIC POET OF
THE EXILE (SECOND ISAIAH)

Suggested Scripture Readings:

Isaiah 40–48
Isaiah 49–55

It may come as a surprise, but the Bible gives us no account whatsoever of the daily life of the Judahites in captivity. We have some detailed, narrative information of what went before (2 Kings and Jeremiah), and we have detailed information of what followed (Ezra and Nehemiah). What we know of the captivity we learn by implication from some of the prophetic oracles of Jeremiah and Ezekiel, and from the unnamed poet of the exile whom we know as Deutero-Isaiah, or Second Isaiah. The oracles of Second Isaiah begin in chapter 40 with the words:

> Comfort, O comfort my people,
>   says your God.
> Speak tenderly to Jerusalem and cry to her
>   that she has served her term,
> that she has received from the LORD's hand
>   double for all her sins (40:1–2),

and continue through chapter 55, ending with descriptive words of the joyful trip home to Judah:

> For you shall go out in joy,
>> and be led back in peace;
> the mountains and the hills before you shall burst into song,
>> and all the trees of the field shall clap their hands.
> Instead of the thorn shall come up the cypress;
>> instead of the brier shall come up the myrtle;
> and it shall be to the LORD for a memorial,
>> for an everlasting sign that shall not be cut off (55:12–13).

We know very little about Second Isaiah, not even his name. There are some hints about him in his oracles. His call as a prophet may be seen in his prologue, chapter 40. In response to a voice which commands "Cry out," he responds:

> "What shall I cry?"
> All the people are grass,
>> their constancy is like the flower of the field,
> the grass withers, the flower fades,
>> when the breath of the LORD blows upon it (40:6–7).

The oracles of Second Isaiah are so strong and optimistic that we are apt to forget that he too was a captive person, and that he too had reason for despair. After his call he could look back on his former feelings, before his call, and say with Ezekiel, "I sat there among them" (Ez 3:15).

Changes in Tone and Content from First Isaiah

When students and readers make their way through the book of Isaiah, as they arrive at the oracles of Second Isaiah they become aware of many changes in tone and content. (a) The fear-inspiring military giant from the east, Assyria, is not mentioned in the oracles of Second Isaiah.[1] (b) Jerusalem is in ruins (52:9) and is a place to look forward to returning to. (c) The preservation of the house of David, with which Isaiah was preoccupied, is not a concern of Second Isaiah. The only time David is mentioned is to declare that the former covenant with David is now made with the people of Yahweh. (d) The tone encountered is one of complete joy. In fact joy is demanded:

> Sing, O heavens, for the LORD has done it;
>> shout, O depths of the earth;
> break forth into singing, O mountains,
>> O forest, and every tree in it (44:23).

(e) This prophet does not address the powerful decision makers of

Israel, as the eighth century prophets had, but addresses the people as a whole:

> Comfort, O comfort my people,
>   says your God (40:1).

(f) There is an emphasis on new developments in history and theology. A new and different age is about to begin:

> See, the former things have come to pass,
>   and new things I now declare (42:9).

> I am about to do a new thing (43:19).

> From this time forward I make you hear new things (48:6).

(g) There is a new political and military leader in the world, Cyrus, who will fulfill the will of Yahweh as he subdues the nations, including Babylon, which had been used to punish Israel.

> "He is my shepherd, and he shall carry out my purpose." . . .
> Thus says the LORD to his anointed, to Cyrus, whose right hand I have grasped to subdue the nations before him and strip kings of their robes (44:28–45:1).

(h) There are no autobiographical references such as we find scattered throughout First Isaiah.

Israel in Captivity

Second Isaiah addressed a captive people, unified by a common past and present condition, who had passed through a period of horror, followed by decades of despair and despondency. They were a small, powerless people, buried in the midst of a mighty and rich empire. This empire was located in a center of ancient civilization and had an ornate, pompous and mythological religion, rich in ritual and astronomy and mythological folklore. With the background of the destruction of the temple of Yahweh, the city of Jerusalem, and the apparent termination of the house of David, the theologians and priests of Israel had many questions to ponder. To assist them they had the writings of the eighth century prophets, including Isaiah, and the first edition of the Deuteronomistic History (Joshua, Judges, Samuel, Kings). They also had a collection of Psalms from the temple of David, and these Psalms would provide the form for many of the oracles of Second Isaiah. Much of the diction of the Psalms is found in Second Isaiah.[2]

We know that they were granted a certain amount of freedom. They were able to work for wages and participate in the market.

> Why do you spend your money for that which is not bread,
> and your labor for that which does not satisfy (55:2)?

We have reason to believe that they were able to meet together to study and discuss their scriptures, and, happily, new scriptures were expanded by priests, scribes, and at least one major new prophet. They were able to write and receive letters from what was left of Judah. In the early days of captivity Jeremiah had written to them, saying:

> Build houses and live in them; plant gardens and eat their produce. Take wives and have sons and daughters . . . multiply there, and do not decrease (Jer 29:5).

It is possible, both because of the new emphasis on writings in the Judahite community, and because the captivity people may not have had a public forum, that Second Isaiah may have been a prophet who was basically a writer instead of a public preacher, and that his oracles were passed from gathering to gathering, from congregation to congregation to be read. But this is only speculation.

The Division of Second Isaiah

The second section of Isaiah consists of fifteen chapters, divided as follows:

Prologue	Chapter 40
Hope for Israel	Chapters 41–47
Hope for Zion	Chapters 48–54
Postlude	Chapter 55

Both the prologue and the postlude are hymns of praise and hope for salvation, stressing the power of God's word over everything.

God's word is not the *written* word, but the word which comes forth from God, in other words, *his will.*[3]

For a substantial introductory discussion of the themes and content of Second Isaiah, we recommend *Reading the Old Testament,* by Lawrence Boadt (Paulist Press), pp. 416 through 430. Father Boadt writes, "The language soars on long strings of adjectives and titles for God. It is filled with images of rebuilding, restoring, renewing, and recreating."[4]

Examining the body of these oracles, scholars have differed as to whether they consist of many small pearls, strung together like beads in a necklace, or whether there are a small number of longer poems.[5] A difference in feeling has been noticed in the early oracles (chapters 41–48) and the later oracles (chapters 49–54). The addressees in the early oracles are Israel/Jacob. Beginning with chapter 49 the addressees are frequently Zion/Jerusalem. In the commentary on Isaiah in *The New Jerome Biblical Commentary,*[6] Carroll Stuhlmueller writes, "Chapter 49 marks a serious shift in the preaching of Dt-Isa and in the organization of the book. . . . The confidence [of the earlier section] modulates into a contemplative or somber attitude toward suffering and rejection."[7] Stuhlmueller sees autobiographical material in the opening words of chapter 49:

> The LORD called me before I was born,
>   while I was in my mother's womb he named me. . . .
> But I said, "I have labored in vain,
>   I have spent my strength for nothing and vanity;
>   yet surely my cause is with the LORD" (49:1,4).

It has been suggested that the early oracles were written before the defeat of Babylon by Cyrus, and of course before the issuance of his edict which ended the first phase of captivity for the Judahites:

> "Thus says King Cyrus of Persia: The LORD, the God of Heaven, has given me all the kingdoms of the earth, and he has charged me to build him a house at Jerusalem in Judah. Any of those among you who are of his people . . . are now permitted to go up to Jerusalem in Judah, and rebuild the house of the LORD, the God of Israel" (Ezr 1:2).

So the early period was a time of expectation, a captive community on the verge of liberation.

The oracles found in chapters 49–54 may reflect conflict and practical disputes which developed after the first returnees arrived in Jerusalem. After the early returnees arrived in Jerusalem, reality settled in, and it is without doubt that theological conflict played a role in tempering the unbridled joy and hope of the recently released captive community. There were many practical, down to earth problems to be dealt with, and there were conflicting viewpoints, both theologically and logistically. It is not our purpose to explore this period in detail. We know that there were hard feelings in the restored community between those who returned from captivity and those who had never been carried away. It is also possible that early returnees had conflicts with those who arrived home later. And we should remind ourselves that there was no supreme council on orthodoxy to settle theological disputes concerning the role of the temple, the place of written scrolls, the identity of the community, the place of ritual, the definition of law, and so forth. There is no doubt that there were power struggles in the rebuilt Jerusalem. It is possible that these disputes affected the later oracles of Second Isaiah, who may have been influenced by the ancient levitical priesthood (the Deuteronomists) whose ideas were opposed by the viewpoint of a competitive priesthood known as the Aaronides.

The change in tone can be summarized in this way. The later oracles of Deutero-Isaiah found in chapters 49–54 come from a transition period between the unbridled hope of the early oracles (40–48), written before the final defeat of Babylon and the edict of Cyrus, and the down-to-earth, practical problems dealt with in the oracles called Trito-Isaiah, written in Jerusalem after the captivity had terminated.

The Puzzle of the Servant Songs in Second Isaiah

Even an introductory appraisal of Second Isaiah must include comments concerning the much studied passages called the "servant songs." The identity of the servant is one of the most fascinating problems of the study of the Hebrew Bible. In the New Testament era it had already been studied and debated for centuries. In Acts 8:34, after reading from one of the servant songs, an Ethiopian eunuch asks Philip:

> About whom may I ask does the prophet say this, about himself or about someone else?

There are four servant passages in Second Isaiah: 42:1–4, 49:1–6, 50:4–9, 52:13–53:12. The third song begins with the words:

The Lord God has given me the tongue of a teacher,
  that I may know how to sustain the weary with a word.
Morning by morning he wakens,
  wakens my ear to listen to those who are taught.
The Lord God has opened my ear, and I was not rebellious,
  I did not turn backward.
I gave my back to those who struck me
  and my cheeks to those who pulled out the beard;
I did not hide my face from insult and spitting (50:4–6).

There have been two types of scholarly interpretation concerning the identity of the servant, collective and individual. Collective theories have included the nation Israel, a small part of the nation Israel—faithful believers—and an idealized Israel. Individual theories have included Moses, Isaiah, Jeremiah, Deutero-Isaiah, Cyrus, Zerubbabel, Jehoiakin, a symbolic king, and a future unknown person.[8]

Two interesting observations have been made by many scholars concerning the location of the servant songs in the canonical text. (1) If the servant songs are removed from the text, and the text joined together, there is no evidence of their having been removed, and, on the contrary, the text has a smoother logical development. (2) When the servant songs are joined together they seem to have their own, step by step, theological development. In light of these two facts we believe that the servant songs had an origin separate from the other oracles attributed to Second Isaiah. In light of the tremendous amount of serious and exhausting study applied to these passages, and readily available to the student of any level, we will limit our discussion. Our best guess is that the servant may be an idealized figure, representative of Israel, or a holy community within Israel (a called out group) with a mission to Israel and ultimately the whole world:

. . . so he shall startle many nations;
  kings shall shut their mouths because of him (Is 52:15).[9]

Universalism and Other Profound Themes in Second Isaiah

There are many profound themes in Second Isaiah which deserve our attention, but which we can only mention. The Judahite community in captivity experienced a widening of theological views which would not have been possible if the people of Yahweh had remained members of a Jerusalem-bound cult. Here are some of these areas of perception and growth. (1) A universalism of Yahweh's reign, which had its roots in the oracles of Isaiah of Jerusalem, permeated the oracles of Second Isaiah:

> Even the nations are like a drop in the bucket,
>   and are accounted as dust on the scales. . . .
> All the nations are as nothing before him;
>   they are accounted by him as less than nothing and emptiness
>   (40:15,17).

(2) Yahweh is declared as the creator of the world, the Lord

> who created the heavens and stretched them out,
>   who spread out the earth and what comes from it,
> who gives breath to the people upon it
>   and spirit to those who walk in it (42:5).

The Hebrew word for create, *bara*, is found sixteen times in Second Isaiah. (3) The people in captivity began to revive their interest in an ancient pre-monarchical tradition, the exodus. Second Isaiah, and other theologians of the captivity period, were able to nourish the ancient exodus tradition and bring it to the mature, central, and vital place it now occupies in the Hebrew Bible. (4) The use of idols by the Babylonians and others comes in for special attack.

> . . . they hire a goldsmith, who makes it [gold] into a god;
>   then they fall down and worship!
> They lift it to their shoulders, they carry it,
>   they set it in its place, and it stands there;
>   it cannot move from its place.
> If one cries out to it, it does not answer
>   or save anyone from trouble (46:6–7).

Conclusion

We have briefly reviewed the outline of the oracles ascribed to an unnamed exilic prophet whose oracles became an extension of the oracles of Isaiah of Jerusalem. We remember that the first thirty-nine chapters of Isaiah did not exist as a separate scroll when Second Isaiah took form. We do not know the exact details concerning the emer-

gence of the canonical book, but we have noted some influences of
Second Isaiah in the earlier chapters of Isaiah. In our closing chapter
(17) we will discuss Second Isaiah further as we look at the unity of
the canonical book. Before that we will briefly review the section of
Isaiah called Trito-Isaiah.

STUDY QUESTIONS

1. Identify six changes encountered when a reader moves from read-
    ing First Isaiah and begins Second Isaiah.

2. What are our sources of information about life in captivity for the
    Judahite community?

3. What change takes place in the oracles of Second Isaiah beginning
    with chapter 49, and how do we account for the change?

4. What are two types of interpretation related to the identification
    of the servant of the Lord? Give examples of each.

5. Name three profound theological themes found in Second Isaiah
    which developed during the captivity period?

NOTES

1. Assyria is mentioned one time in 52:4, but this is a prose, editorial addition to the oracles of Second Isaiah.

2. Claus Westermann, *Isaiah 40–66* (Philadelphia: Westminster,
1969), p. 41. It is also possible that the oracles of Second Isaiah influenced the language of Psalms written later.

3. Gerhard Von Rad has a beautiful discussion of the word of the
Lord in his *Old Testament Theology, Volume II* (New York: Harper
and Row, 1965), pp. 80–98, where he identifies the oldest utterance
of the prophets as the words attributed to Elijah, that there should be
neither dew nor rain in Israel "except by my word." He also discusses
the use of the term "word of the Lord" in Deutero-Isaiah
(pp. 93–94).

4. Lawrence Boadt, *Reading the Old Testament* (Mahwah: Paulist
Press, 1984), pp. 416–417.

5. *Reading the Old Testament*, p. 418.

6. I highly recommend to the serious student of Isaiah a complete reading of the commentary on "Deutero-Isaiah and Trito-Isaiah" by Carroll Stuhlmueller, C.P., in *The New Jerome Biblical Commentary* (Englewood Cliffs: Prentice Hall, 1990), pp. 329–348.

7. *NJBC*, cited above, p. 339.

8. Consult *Reading the Old Testament*, cited above, pp. 427–430, and the *NJBC*, also cited above, pp. 330–331. For an interesting summary of the symbolic king theory, see J. Alberto Soggin, *Introduction to the Old Testament* (Philadelphia: Westminster, 1976), pp. 314–315.

9. The early Christian church interpreted the work of Jesus as the fulfillment of the servant passages in Isaiah. It is possible that earlier in the first century Paul identified himself as the servant in his mission to the Gentiles. Read Acts 13:47, Galatians 1:15, and Romans 15:21.

Chapter 16

THIRD ISAIAH:
A POST-EXILIC COLLECTION

Suggested Scripture Reading:

Isaiah 56–66

As you progress through the book of Isaiah, when you read the opening verses of chapter 56, you know you are in a different time and a different place.

> Thus says the LORD:
> Maintain justice and do right,
>   for soon my salvation will come, and my deliverance be
>   revealed.
> Happy is the mortal who does this,
>   the one who holds it fast,
> who keeps the sabbath, not profaning it,
>   and refrains from doing any evil (56:1–2).

The editor who arranged for this oracle to begin what scholars have called Third Isaiah knew what he was doing. He couldn't have made his point better if he had whacked us with a board. We are no longer under the influence of the powerful, moving, uplifting words of faith delivered by Second Isaiah. Beginning with chapter 56 there is a difference in tone and viewpoint. The opening passionless oracle, for one thing, mentions keeping the sabbath, a word which does not appear in Second Isaiah (or First Isaiah either). Where are we?

    We are in post-exilic Jerusalem. Some exiles have arrived from

Babylon. And there are many problems, economic, social, and religious.

Studying Isaiah is like mountain climbing. As you slowly make your way up the slopes of the mountain (chapters 1–39) you encounter interesting challenges and experience many satisfying experiences. Each foot of progress is a reward, and you are never bored (well, some of us feel that way anyway). When you reach the summit (chapters 40–55) you are overcome with excitement. Unlimited horizons are everywhere. You are left breathless. You are hardly conscious of your many pains as you scale the beauty of exalted nature.

But you have to come back to ground level, where the problems of everyday life resume (chapters 56–66). This is the collection of oracles gathered together in post-exilic Jerusalem.

The title Third Isaiah is misleading. Because the original prophet Isaiah of Jerusalem was a person, and Second Isaiah was a person, we expect Third Isaiah to be a person. It is better to think of the last section of Isaiah as a collection of oracles. The date for these oracles is usually given as 540–500 B.C.E. Although the collection has an uninspiring start, all is not lost. Some of the oracles are prosaic, mundane, and even annoying. Others, however, are affirmative, uplifting, and inspiring. For example in chapter 61 we have passages worthy of Second Isaiah.

> The spirit of the LORD is upon me,
>   because the LORD has anointed me,
> he has sent me to bring good news to the oppressed,
>   to bind up the brokenhearted,
> to proclaim liberty to the captives,
>   and release to the prisoners (61:1).

In fairness, chapters 60 through 62 are inspiring chapters, and it is even possible that these chapters may have been written by Second Isaiah after he returned to Jerusalem. Although scholars can see stylistic and verbal differences, this could be accounted for by a change in environment and the passage of years. Another chapter of note is chapter 66 (1–13), a powerful passage in its Deuteronomistic thrust.

Problems in Post-Exilic Jerusalem

We have already referred to problems among the inhabitants of post-exilic Jerusalem, conflicts between groups such as those who returned early from captivity and those who returned later. There were other conflicts, conflicts between those who never went into captivity, those who returned from Egypt or other places, and those who lived in the territory who were not, or were not considered, Judahites or people of Israel.

There were economic hardships and devastation everywhere. In an oracle of the prophet Haggai dated 520[1] we read this description:

> Consider how you have fared. You have sown much, and harvested little; you eat, but you never have enough; you drink, but you never have your fill; you clothe yourselves, but no one is warm; and you that earn wages earn wages to put them into a bag with holes (Hag 1:6).

There were also various types of theological conflict. One of these conflicts was reminiscent of an earlier documented conflict between competing priesthoods in the pre-exilic days of King Josiah, set forth in this passage:

> Whoever slaughters an ox is like one who kills a human being;
>   whoever sacrifices a lamb, like one who breaks a dog's neck;
> whoever presents a grain offering, like one who offers swine's
>   blood;
>   whoever makes a memorial offering of frankincense like one
>   who blesses an idol (66:3).

This passage (read vv. 3–4) is similar in viewpoint to similar passages in Isaiah 1:11–17 and Amos 5:21–24, and represents the viewpoint of the levitical priesthood (all priests in Deuteronomy are Levites) in opposition to the Aaronide priesthood which produced the so-called Priestly documents. A second conflict is revealed when Third Isaiah speaks about extending the priesthood by suggesting that foreigners could become priests:

> I am coming to gather all nations and tongues. . . . And I will also take some of them as priests and as Levites (66:18 and 21),

when Ezekiel had stated that only descendants of Zadok could serve as priests (Ez 44:15–16). And a third conflict is referenced in chapter 60 where foreigners are welcomed to the temple and take part in rebuilding Jerusalem. This is contrary to a position later taken in the book of Ezra (4:13). And the list goes on.

The Chiastic Structure of Third Isaiah

Third Isaiah, like First Isaiah, contains both oracles of hope and oracles of stern rebuke. But the arrangement is not simply one of alternation such as we frequently found in the first section of Isaiah. Instead scholars have discovered a symmetrical pattern for the arrangement of the book, called chiasm (see the chart in our chapter 12 defining and illustrating an example of chiasm). In the middle of Third Isaiah we find three chapters (60–62) of exalted poetry which could be called "The gospel of peace and prosperity for Jerusalem." In these chapters the hearers are told that days of glory are coming for them when they will no longer be oppressed and brokenhearted, but will be proud to be known as "priests of the LORD, and ministers of our God." The day is coming when Jerusalem will know nothing but prosperity, peace, recognition, glory, righteousness.

Around this center twelve clusters of oracles are symmetrically arranged so as to correspond. Six come before the center, and six follow the center in reverse order.[2]

Good news (for foreigners)	56:2–8
Judgment on corrupt leaders	56:9–57:13
Salvation for the people	57:14–21
False worship	58:1–4
Lament and confession	59:1–15
The Lord's action	59:16–20

Following these six clusters of oracles, the gospel of peace and prosperity for Jerusalem is contained in the three chapters, 60–62. Then the reverse order is noted as below:

The Lord's action	63:1–6
Lament and confession	63:7–64:12
False worship	65:1–16
Salvation for the people	65:17–25
Judgment on corrupt leaders	66:1–6
Good news (including foreigners)	66:10–23

Although the chiastic structure is not air-tight, the intention of the editor is obvious, and being aware of it assists us in understanding a facet of the mind of the ancient scribes.

Theological Themes of Third Isaiah

We will summarize several important themes presented by Third Isaiah. (1) In the eighth century and the seventh century, the whole nation was punished because of the sins of the leaders. This is no longer true. Now, if part of the community is faithful, and part is wicked, the faithful will be saved.

> So I will do for my servants' sake
>   and not destroy them all.
> I will bring forth descendants from Jacob,
>   and from Judah inheritors of my mountains;
>   my chosen shall inherit it,
>   and my servants shall settle there (65:8–9).

Implicit in the oracles of Third Isaiah is that the faithless will be punished but the faithful will be blessed. This is a development of the Deuteronomic theme of blessings and curses individualized.[3] It is also a development of the remnant theme of First Isaiah.

(2) There is a joyful universalism in Third Isaiah.

> And the foreigners who join themselves to the LORD to minister to him, to love the name of the LORD, and to be his servants . . . their burnt offerings and their sacrifices will be accepted on my altar; for my house shall be called a house of prayer for all peoples (56:6–8).

The universalism of Third Isaiah is different from the universalism of Deutero-Isaiah. In chapters 40 to 55, the universalism referred to is the control of Yahweh over the military victories of Babylon, for judgment on Israel, and Persia, for judgment on Babylon. In Third Isaiah, universalism refers to foreign nations honoring Yahweh and his people, coming to Jerusalem and worshiping the Lord, and sharing the blessing of God's people.

> Nations shall come to your light,
>   and kings to the brightness of your dawn (60:3).

(3) While there is a great emphasis in Third Isaiah on the restoration of Jerusalem and the cult of Yahweh and the temple, there is a Deuteronomistic interpretation of the role of the temple in the words, *My house shall be a house of prayer* (56:7). Influenced by the

eighth century prophets and Jeremiah, there is a de-emphasis on ritual and sacrifice and an emphasis on righteous living:

> For I the LORD love justice,
>   I hate robbery and wrongdoing (61:8).

Yahweh did not dwell in the temple, but in the heavens. He is not
pictured, as in Haggai, distressed over the delay in the building of the
temple.

> Thus says the LORD:
> Heaven is my throne and the earth is my footstool;
>   what is the house that you would build for me,
>   and what is my resting place?
> All these things my hand has made
>   and so all things are mine, says the LORD (66:1–2).

While it is important to keep the sabbath as a sign of honor to Yahweh,
and for humanitarian reasons (Deut 5:12–15), there is no interest in
the details of worship related to the sacrificial system.

Conclusion

Third Isaiah (56–66) continues some of the joy of Deutero-Isaiah
with uplifting songs of salvation, but there is a somber background of
conflict and frustration. The political and economic realities of a frag-
mented society, and the power struggles of conflicting groups linger
close to the surface of the text. Nevertheless this section of scripture
is vitally important. It is reported that Jesus quoted from Third Isaiah
when he drove the money changers from the temple:

> Is it not written, "My house shall be called a house of prayer
> for all nations" (Mk 11:17)?

And we remember that Jesus read from Third Isaiah when he began
his public ministry in the synagogue of Nazareth:

> The Spirit of the LORD is upon me,
>   because he has anointed me to bring good news to the poor.
> He has sent me to proclaim release to the captives
>   and recovery of sight to the blind,

to let the oppressed go free,
   to proclaim the year of the Lord's favor (Lk 4:18–19).

STUDY QUESTIONS

1. What are some differences in environment which we notice when we arrive at chapter 56 of Isaiah?

2. Why do you think there is no mention of the sabbath by First Isaiah or Second Isaiah?

3. Give three examples of theological conflicts in post-exilic Jerusalem hinted at in Third Isaiah.

4. What was the attitude of Third Isaiah toward foreigners?

5. Explain the structural arrangement of the oracles of Third Isaiah.

6. What is the difference between the universalism of Second Isaiah and Third Isaiah?

7. What was the attitude of Third Isaiah concerning the temple?

NOTES

1. For this date see *The Interpreter's One-Volume Bible Commentary*, and *The New Jerome Biblical Commentary*.

2. This chiastic arrangement is explained thoroughly by Norman Gottwald in his book *The Hebrew Bible: A Socio-Literary Introduction* (Philadelphia: Westminster, 1985), pp. 506–509.

3. Read Deuteronomy 27 and 28.

Chapter 17

THE UNITY OF THE BOOK OF ISAIAH

In our quest to understand any part of the books of the Hebrew Bible it is helpful to know who the author was, the circumstances of the author, and the time of writing. Knowing that the book of Isaiah had at least four authors and that it reached its canonical form as the end result of a developmental process which spanned centuries makes it impossible for the serious student to ignore the stages of the process. But there is one stage which we could inadvertently overlook if we become entirely involved in the process. That is the final stage. Scholars have reminded us that it was as a complete scroll that the church admitted the book of Isaiah to the canon.

Someone, or some group, was responsible for bringing together the various parts and strands of Isaiah, producing the magnificent book which has had such a profound impact on its readers for more than two thousand years. Among other things, Isaiah is a great work of religious art, carefully and lovingly put together and unified with cords, strands and themes which run throughout the book. Like a great piece of orchestral music, Isaiah has many voices, tempos, and themes, themes which are sometimes introduced briefly by one voice to be later restated by other instruments, sometimes in unison, sometimes in harmony, sometimes softly (*pianissimo*) and sometimes in full volume (*fortissimo*).

The Structure of the Book

Looking at the structure of this work we have noted that there are three movements like the three movements of a great concerto.

For the solo voice we look to the spirit of Yahweh. Some of the symmetrical structure is clear to us. In an early edition of Isaiah's oracles (chapters 2–12) we noted that in the center of this collection the memoirs of Isaiah (6–8:18) have been inserted. In Second Isaiah (40–55) we find in the approximate center the passage which announces the role of Cyrus the Persian as the instrument of Yahweh (44:28–45:7). In Third Isaiah (56–66) we find, at the center, three glorious songs of salvation (60–62), possibly composed by the majestic poet/prophet of the exile.

Major Themes Throughout the Book

There are several unifying themes which run throughout the book. The title *The Holy One of Israel* expresses the center of Isaiah's theology and has its roots in Isaiah's vision of Yahweh in the temple (chapter 6). Perhaps we will hear a reminder of the three-part structure of Isaiah in the cry of the seraphs:

Holy, holy, holy is the LORD of hosts;
    the whole earth is full of his glory (6:3).

Here also is a statement of the universalism of Yahweh which is an important theme throughout the book.

In examining the meaning of the title *The Holy One of Israel* we always look at the first and last words. Let's not ignore the central word in English, *One*.

Hear, O Israel: The LORD is our God, the LORD alone (Deut 6:4).

Yahweh is the one God for Israel. As the student continues his or her way through the book of Isaiah he or she will have an appreciation of the development of monotheism in the religion of Judah as expressed in the various forms of universalism which we have noted in all three sections of the book of Isaiah. For Second Isaiah there is no god to compare with Yahweh. He alone is the creator of the heavens and the earth and the Lord of history.

The title *The Holy One of Israel* appears twenty-seven times in Isaiah, and only a few times outside of Isaiah.[1]

Another strong theme which runs throughout the canonical book

PROPHETIC CONCEPTS AND POETIC IMAGES OF FIRST ISAIAH

Repeated in Second Isaiah and/or Third Isaiah Which Indicate Extent of Editorial Activity in the Production of the Canonical Version of the Book of Isaiah

FIRST ISAIAH Chapters 1–39 (Jerusalem)	SECOND ISAIAH Chapters 40–55 (Babylon)	THIRD ISAIAH Chapters 56–66 (Jerusalem)
Holy One of Israel 1:4, 5:24	Holy One of Israel 47:4, 49:7	Holy One of Israel 60:9, 60:14
Build a highway 11:16	Build a highway 40:3	Build a highway 62:10
Blindness of rulers 6:10	Blindness of rulers 43:8	Blindness of rulers 56:10
Jerusalem restored 2:2–3	Jerusalem restored 40:1, 44:28	Jerusalem restored 62:1
Idols and images 10:10, 14	Idols and images 44:9–20	Idols and images 57:13
Darkness and light 9:2	Darkness and light 42:16	Darkness and light 59:9
Prisoners 14:17	Prisoners 49:9	Prisoners 61:1
Bloody vengeance for Edom chapter 34		Bloody vengeance for Edom chapter 63
Briers and thorns 5:6, 7:23	Thorns and briers 55:13	
Critique of sacrificial System 1:11–17		Critique of sacrificial System 66:3–4
Jackals, ostriches 13:21–22	Jackals, ostriches 43:20	
Wolf and the lamb 11:6		Wolf and the lamb 65:25
Foreigners coming to Jerusalem 2:2–3		Foreigners coming to Jerusalem 56:6–7, 60:3
Social justice 1:17		Social justice 56:1, 61:8
Trees exulting 14:8	Trees exulting 55:12	
Potter and clay 29:16		Potter and clay 64:8
Empty houses 5:9		Inhabited houses 65:21
Using foreign power (Assyria) 10:5	Using foreign power (Persia) 44:28	

is the centrality of Jerusalem. To cite just a few of numerous examples, in chapter 2 we read:

> For out of Zion shall go forth instruction,
>   and the word of the LORD from Jerusalem (2:3).

In Second Isaiah Jerusalem is the city to return to and to rebuild. In Third Isaiah we read:

> For Zion's sake I will not keep silent,
>   and for Jerusalem's sake I will not rest,
> until her vindication shines out like the dawn,
>   and her salvation like a burning torch (62:1).

In our first chapter we discussed the role of Jerusalem in the development of the Hebrew Bible. There is no doubt that the growth of the oracles of Isaiah into the longest book of the Bible was influenced by his being the only eighth century prophet to live in Jerusalem and to have as a major concern the welfare of the city chosen by Yahweh.

Repeated Themes

From the many themes which run through more than one section of the book and unite the various sections we will point out ten, using a method employed by Isaiah of Jerusalem—the list.

(1) The theme of Yahweh using the foreign nations to accomplish his judgment is obvious in both Isaiah and Second Isaiah. In Isaiah Assyria is used to punish Israel, and in Second Isaiah Persia is used to punish Babylon.

(2) The theme of a special highway is found in all three sections. The highway in Isaiah is from Assyria (11:16) for a remnant of Israel. For Second Isaiah the highway is through the desert for our God (40:3), but in chapter 35, attributed to or at least influenced by Second Isaiah, the highway is for the redeemed of the Lord (35:8). In Third Isaiah we read:

> . . . prepare the way for the people;
> build up, build up the highway,
>   clear it of stones (62:10).

(3) The famous passage of Isaiah of the wolf and the lamb lying

down together (11:6) along with the conclusion is repeated in Third
Isaiah:

> The wolf and the lamb shall feed together,
> the lion shall eat straw like the ox . . .
> They shall not hurt or destroy
> in all my holy mountain, says the LORD (65:25).

Here we have an example of a prophet quoting an earlier prophet.

(4) Isaiah frequently used the expression "briers and thorns" to
describe the land on which the judgment of Yahweh had come (5:6;
7:23; 27:4). This figure is reversed by Second Isaiah.

> Instead of the thorn shall come up the cypress;
> instead of the brier shall come up the myrtle (55:13).

(5) In describing destroyed cities Isaiah said they would be in-
habited by *jackals* and *ostriches* (13:21–22; 34:13). Second Isaiah
writes, "The wild animals will honor me, the jackals and the ostriches" (43:20).

(6) Isaiah mentioned houses without inhabitants (5:9) but Third
Isaiah says, "They shall build houses and inhabit them" (65:21).

(7) One of the earliest themes in Isaiah is that of foreigners coming to the house of the Lord (2:3). It is also one of the last themes in
Third Isaiah:

> I am coming to gather all nations and tongues;
> and they shall come and see my glory (66:18).

(8) Another early theme which is repeated late in the book is the
critique of the sacrificial system. The passage in Isaiah begins with the
words, "What to me is the multitude of your sacrifices?" (Is 1:11). In
Third Isaiah a passage with a similar viewpoint is recorded in 66:3–4.

(9) The theme of social justice which appears in Isaiah 1–5 reappears as a major theme in Third Isaiah. While the language of the final
section of Isaiah is abstract and stilted, nevertheless the theme
is there.

> Maintain justice, and do what is right (56:1).

> For I the LORD love justice,
> I hate robbery and wrongdoing (61:8).

If you offer your food to the hungry
   and satisfy the needs of the afflicted,
then your light shall rise in the darkness,
   and your gloom like the noonday (58:10).

(10) The theme of blindness as an image of resistance to Yahweh's truth appears in all three sections. Isaiah is told at the time of his call that his words to *this people* would result in their being unable to see with their eyes. Second Isaiah writes:

Bring forth the people who are blind yet have eyes (43:8),

and Third Isaiah says of Jerusalem's corrupt rulers, "Israel's sentinels are blind."

The Concept of Faith in Isaiah

No summary of Isaiah would be complete without reference to Isaiah's seminal concept of faith. In 735 Jerusalem and the house of David were threatened by an anti-Assyrian coalition consisting of Syria and Ephraim (Israel).

When the house of David heard that Aram had allied itself
with Ephraim the heart of Ahaz and the heart of his people
shook as the trees of the forest shake before the wind (Is 7:2).

Isaiah, like Hosea, did not believe in foreign alliances. To ally with a military power for protection (in this case against Assyria) was considered by Isaiah as a betrayal of Israel's ancient faith in Yahweh as the protector of his people. Isaiah told Ahaz to have faith in Yahweh.

Take heed, be quiet, do not fear,
   and do not let your heart be faint. . . .
If you do not stand firm in faith,
   you shall not stand (Is 7:4,9).

Isaiah encouraged Ahaz to maintain a position of neutrality. This may be the earliest written, historical example of faith in the Hebrew Bible.[2] The profoundest answer to the question "Why should Judah trust Yahweh?" became part of the book of Isaiah, the part we know as Second Isaiah. Yahweh is the controller of history. Yahweh is the creator. Yahweh has not forgotten his people Israel. He will bring them home. He had disciplined them and now they were forgiven.

> For a brief moment I abandoned you,
>   but with great compassion I will gather you.
> In overflowing wrath for a moment I hid my face from you,
>   but with everlasting love I will have compassion on you,
>   says the LORD, your redeemer (54:7–8).

There are probably many who think that Isaiah's isolationist outlook was very impractical and naive. But several things can be said. Judah did outlast Israel by more than a century, and second, and far more important, Isaiah's seminal concept of faith has continued to grow, and thousands of years later it finds itself at the center of the religion of God's people.

STUDY QUESTIONS

1. Locate a passage in all three sections of Isaiah referring to the centrality of Jerusalem.

2. What kinds of tasks would the final editor of the canonical book of Isaiah have performed?

3. The author has suggested that the book of Isaiah resembles a work of great orchestral music. What did he have in mind by this comparison?

4. Discuss Isaiah's concept of faith and give a concrete example.

5. How did Yahweh use foreign nations to accomplish his will in First Isaiah and Second Isaiah?

6. Locate a reference to a divine highway in all three sections of Isaiah.

7. What famous passage from Third Isaiah (quoted by Jesus) is similar to the passage found in First Isaiah, chapter 2:2–3?

8. In order for monotheism to emerge, the God of Israel had to be perceived as universal. What passages in Isaiah describe or refer to this universalism?

NOTES

1. The title *Holy One of Israel* appears twelve times in chapters 1–39 and thirteen times in chapters 40–55. It appears two times in chapters 56–66.

2. This seminal concept of faith, trusting in Yahweh for deliverance, grew and matured in the following development of Judah's history. It became so strong and so basic that it was projected into Israel's past as a common understanding of the behavior of Israel's patriarchs, pre-monarchical leaders, judges and early kings. It became part of the written scriptures after the emergence of the book of Isaiah. The books of the Bible which now appear in the tetrateuch (Genesis through Numbers) did not appear in their final form until the sixth or fifth century.

FOR FURTHER READING

Ackroyd, Peter R. "The Book of Isaiah," *The Interpreter's One-Volume Commentary on the Bible*. Nashville: Abingdon, 1971.

Boadt, Lawrence. *Reading the Old Testament, An Introduction*. Mahwah: Paulist Press, 1984.

———. "Ezekiel," *The New Jerome Biblical Commentary*. Englewood Cliffs: Prentice Hall, 1990.

Clements, R.E. "Isaiah, 1–39," *The New Century Bible Commentary*. Grand Rapids: Eerdmans, 1987.

Collins, John J. "Isaiah," *Collegeville Bible Commentary*. Collegeville: Liturgical Press, 1986.

Conrad, Edgar W. *Reading Isaiah*. Minneapolis: Fortress Press, 1991.

Coote, Robert. *Amos Among the Prophets*. Philadelphia: Fortress Press, 1981.

Doorly, William J. *Prophet of Justice, Understanding the Book of Amos*. Mahwah: Paulist Press, 1989.

Duhm, Bernhard. *Das Buch Jesaja*. Gottingen: Vanderhoecj and Ruprecht, 1892, 1902.

Fohrer, Georg. *Introduction to the Old Testament*. Nashville: Abingdon, 1968.

Freidman, Richard Elliott. *The Exile and Biblical Narrative*. Chico: Scholars Press, 1981.

Gottwald, Norman K. *The Tribes of Yahweh*. Maryknoll: Orbis Press, 1981.

———. *The Hebrew Bible, A Socio-Literary Introduction*. Philadelphia: Fortress, 1985.

Hayes, John and Hooker, Paul. *A New Chronology for the Kings of Israel and Judah*. Nashville: Abingdon, 1988.

Hayes, John and Irvine, Stuart. *Isaiah, The Eighth Century Prophet: His Times and Preaching.* Nashville: Abingdon, 1987.

Hopkins, David C. *The Highlands of Canaan.* Sheffield: JSOT Press, 1985.

Irvine, Stuart A. *Isaiah, Ahaz, and the Syro-Ephraimitic Crisis.* Atlanta: Scholars Press, 1990.

Jensen, Joseph and Irwin, William. "Isaiah 1–39," *The New Jerome Biblical Commentary.* Englewood Cliffs: Prentice Hall, 1990.

Kaiser, Otto. *Isaiah 1–12.* Philadelphia: Westminster, 1983.

―――. *Isaiah 12–39.* Philadelphia: Westminster, 1974.

Mc Kenzie, John L. *Second Isaiah, Anchor Bible Series.* New York: Doubleday, 1983.

Pritchard, James C. *The Ancient Near East.* Princeton: Princeton University Press, 1958.

―――. *Ancient Near East in Pictures.* Princeton: Princeton University Press, 1969.

Sanders, James A. "Isaiah in Luke." *Interpretation,* April, 1982, Volume XXXVI, number 2.

Sawyer, John F.A. *The Daily Study Bible Series: Isaiah.* Philadelphia: Westminster, 1984.

Soggin, J. Alberto. *Introduction to the Old Testament.* Philadelphia: Westminster Press, 1976.

Stansell, Gary. *Micah and Isaiah, A Form and Tradition Historical Comparison.* Atlanta: Scholars Press, 1988.

Stuhlmueller, Carroll. "Deutero-Isaiah and Trito-Isaiah." *The New Jerome Biblical Commentary.* Englewood Cliffs: Prentice Hall, 1990.

Von Rad, Gerhard. *Deuteronomy, A Commentary.* Philadelphia: Westminster, 1975.

Westermann, Claus. *Isaiah 40–66.* Philadelphia: Westminster, 1969.

Wilson, Robert. *Prophecy and Society in Ancient Israel.* Philadelphia: Westminster, 1984.

Yee, Gale A. *Composition and Tradition in the Book of Hosea, A Redaction Critical Investigation.* New York: Scholars Press, 1987.

INDEX

Aaronide priesthood, 145
accusation of Yahweh's people, 10
Ackroyd, Peter, 59, 79
addressees in divisions of Isaiah, xiv, 111
addressees of Isaiah, 10–11, 32, 44
addressees of Second Isaiah, 134–35
agriculture, metaphor from, 113
Ahaz of Judah, 24, 46, 50–54, 66, 69–70, 115, 155
alliances, opposition to military, 47, 65, 111–12
Amos, parallels with Isaiah, 16
animals as poetic symbols, 82–83
Apocalypse, Little, of Isaiah, 119–23
Apocalypse of Isaiah, 97–107
apocalyptic literature, elements of, 99
Ariel protected, 112–13
Ashdod rebellion, 127
assassination attempt against Ahaz, 66
Asshur, 21
Assyrian aggression, ix
Assyrian characteristics, 22–24

Baasha, house of, 53, 59
Babylon, 120, 122, 135
Babylon, oracle against, 92–94
Babylonian captivity, 133–40
Boadt, Lawrence, 89, 137, 142
briers and thorns, 34, 134, 154
bronze altar, 70

catch-word principle, 72, 110
chapters, divisions in present day Bible, 55
chiasm, example of, 110, 146
city, in apocalypse of Isaiah, 103–04
Clements, Roland, 12, 39, 59, 79, 123
coalition, anti-Assyrian, 24, 44, 47, 64, 115
Coote, Robert, 39, 49
coronation hymn, 74
creation in Second Isaiah, 140
curds and honey, 56, 59
Cyrus the Persian, 135, 137, 151

Damascus, Ahaz's visit to, 70
Daniel, 99–100, 104–05
Davidic (royal) theology, 116
debt slavery, 37

Deutero-Isaiah, x, 133–42, 152
deuteronomistic history (DH), xxii, 51, 124
deuteronomistic characteristics, 127, 134, 147
disciples of Isaiah, 64
divisions of Isaiah, ix
Duhm, Bernhard, xii

earthquake of mid-eighth century, 12, 35
Edom, 119–20
Egypt, alliance with condemned, 111–12
Egypt, oracle against, 88
eighth-century prophets and Isaiah, xv
Elath, seaport of, 47
Eliakim, 94
enthronement hymn, 74, 79
envoys, Babylonian, 126
Esau, 120
Ethiopia, 90
exodus, 4, 140
Ezekiel, 88, 105, 120, 134, 145

faith, defined by Isaiah, 47–48, 51, 114–16, 118, 155–57
foreign nations used by Yahweh, 80, 153
four corners of the earth, 91

geza (Hebrew: stump, stem, root), 81–82
Gottwald, Norman, 149

Haggai, 145
Hayes, John, 12, 44, 49, 58–59, 77, 101, 104
Hezekiah of Judah, 102, 124–32
highway theme, 122, 152–53

historical narratives in Isaiah, 124–32
Holy One of Israel, 11, 43, 112, 151, 157
Hooker, Paul, 79
Hopkins, David, 118
Hosea, 47, 53, 65, 111–13
Hoshea of Israel, 52, 66, 101

illness of Hezekiah, 126, 128
Immanuel, 52–55
Irvine, Stuart, 12, 44, 49, 59, 77, 101, 104

jackals and ostriches, 154
Jeremiah, 89, 136
Jerusalem, historical-theological information, 1–2, 153
Jerusalem, inviolability of, 116–17
Jerusalem, destruction of, 85, 120, 127, 134
Jerusalem after captivity, 138, 143–49
Josiah of Judah, 84–85, 124

Kaiser, Otto, 13, 58, 79, 105
kings, prophets who spoke with, xvi

latifundialization, 37, 39
Leviathan, 99
Levitical priesthood, 145
Lilith, 121
lists, literary form in Isaiah, 32–33, 98
liturgy in Judah, xiv, 76, 89, 101

Maher-shalal-hash-baz, 61–62
marginality, feeling of in Israel, 3
McKenzie, John L., 123
memoirs of Isaiah, 40–59

Menahem, 24, 46, 96
Merodach-baladan, 126–28, 132
minor prophets, xxii
Moab, 88, 101
multiple authors of a Bible book,
    xiii, 150
mythology, Canaanite, 99

nabi (Hebrew: prophet), 67–68,
    127
nations, oracles concerning,
    87–96
new things, theme of, 135
New Testament, Isaiah in the, xi,
    138, 148–49
Nile, oracle against, 88, 90
northern territories of Israel, 78

oracles, arrangements of, 56

past idealized, 16–17
peace, prince of, 73–74
peaceful kingdom, 81–82
Pekah of Israel, 24, 46
pride condemned, 32–33, 80, 85
prism, Sennacherib's, 125
Pul, or Pulu, 93

Rabshakeh, the, 126, 129–30
redaction, exilic, xi, xviii
redaction, stages of, xviii
redactor, Josianic, xviii, 15
relocating populations, 23
remnant, meaning of, 80–81,
    84–85, 147
resurrection, 99, 104–05
Revelation, book of, 100
Rezin of Syria, 24, 46
rod in the hand of Yahweh, 80
royal (Davidic) theology, 4–5,
    116

sabbath, keeping of, 143
sacrificial worship, criticism of,
    13–14, 145
Sargon II, 26, 102–03
scribes, practices of, 8–9
Second Isaiah, x, 133–42, 152
Sennacherib, 3, 12, 26, 125–26,
    128–30
seraphs, 43
servant songs, 138–39, 142
Shalmaneser V, 26, 101–02
Shear-jashub, 49–50
Sidon, merchants of, 90
sight, importance of in Isaiah, 9,
    155
social justice themes, 16, 37, 154
Stuhlmueller, Carroll, 137, 142
stump of Jesse, 81–82
swords into plowshares, 31, 38
Syro-Ephraimitic coalition,
    44–45

Tabeel, son of, 46, 54
Taylor, Colonel R., 125
tetrateuch, 71
Third Isaiah, xii, 143–49, 152
throne names for new king, 75
Tiglath-pileser, 21, 23, 46, 52,
    93
torahs, competing, 15
trade between Assyria and
    Egypt, 102
Trito-Isaiah, xii, 143–49, 152

universalism in Second Isaiah,
    139
universalism in Third Isaiah, 147
universe, ancient view of, 91,
    100
Uriah the priest, 61, 70
Uzziah of Judah, 47

vineyard, song of, 34, 63
vision in the temple, 40–44
visions in apocalyptic literature,
   100

weapons of war, 31
wife of Isaiah, 67
wisdom literature in Isaiah,
   113–14
woes, the seven, 36–37

wolf and the lamb, 82, 153–54
word, of the LORD, 136–37
world, extent of in ancient
   Israel, 91, 100

Yahweh and El, 116, 118
yom kippur, 67

Zaphon, Mount, 91, 95
Zion theology, 5–6, 66, 123